A SHORT HISTORY OF THE

UNIVERSITY OF EDINBURGH

1556–1889

A Short History
of the
UNIVERSITY OF
EDINBURGH

1556–1889

by
D. B. HORN

The
University Press
EDINBURGH

© 1967
EDINBURGH UNIVERSITY PRESS
22 George Square, Edinburgh 8
North America
Aldine Publishing Company
320 West Adams Street, Chicago
Australia & New Zealand
Hodder & Stoughton Ltd
Africa, Oxford University Press
India, P. C. Manaktala & Sons Private Ltd
Far East, M. Graham Brash & Son

Printed in Great Britain
by Thomas Nelson (Printers) Limited
Edinburgh, Scotland

The illustration of the old University buildings
on the half-title of this book
is from an undated painting on the lid of a snuffbox,
reputed to be made from wood of the Tounis College.
This box is in the possession of Mr John Chiene, CA,
to whom the publishers are grateful for allowing them
to reproduce this unique picture.

Preface

In writing a short history of an institution which originated in the second half of the sixteenth century, the basic problems are selection and arrangement of the abundant source material. I was tempted to adopt F. W. Maitland's technique in his *Constitutional history of England* and to write a series of essays which would try to depict the University at various turning-points in its life. In the end it seemed better for a historian who can make no claim to Maitland's genius to adopt a safer if more pedestrian approach by constructing a continuous narrative. This would certainly have been the method used by Principal Robertson, had he ever found leisure and energy to write the history of the University; but none of the University's previous historians has succeeded in writing a history of this kind.

Craufurd and Dalzel were annalists; Bower adopted a topical approach and specialised in biography. The authors of the collection of essays on the history of the University from 1883 to 1933, edited by Logan Turner, tackled the subject by narrating the development of faculties and departments and leaving the work of synthesis to the reader. Indeed, only Grant seriously tried to provide a continuous narrative of significant events, and he virtually gave up the attempt and fell back upon voluminous appendices on detached topics and personalities.

To keep the present work within reasonable limits the subjects selected for continuous treatment have had to be strictly defined and severely pruned. The history of the University Library and Museums comes in only incidentally. The temptation to include much biographical material on Edinburgh principals, professors, and students has had to be resisted. The extremely complicated and obscure problems connected with the origins of the University, which the late Professor Hannay did so much to elucidate, have had to be ignored; I have attempted a fresh account of them in another place. The story of the University's relationship to the other Scottish universities, the church, and the state merits much fuller examination than it receives here. The full treatment of the University's role in the Scottish Enlightenment and its subsequent influence upon Europe and the world would require a book to itself. What then is left? There remains the constitutional and administrative history of the University, including its special relationship to the town council; an account of the University as a teaching institution with some reference to its contributions to scholarship and research; an entirely new history and description of the buildings it occupied down to 1889; and some notes on the social life of regents, professors, and students throughout the centuries.

The *primum mobile* in the writing of this book was our late principal, Sir Edward V. Appleton, who persuaded me to undertake it and, when I hesitated, invoked the authority of the University Court to overcome my doubts. He was energetically supported by the late Professor Croft Dickinson, at that time convener of the Press Committee. My own preference was to confine the narrative to the period of the Tounis College, ending with the Universities (Scotland) Act of 1858, but I have been prevailed upon to go as far as 1889. In spite of his many other commitments, the Secretary to the University, Mr Charles H. Stewart, has agreed to make himself responsible for the more recent history of the University, of which he possesses an unrivalled knowledge. It was to meet him half-way that I agreed to continue the narrative until the passage of the Universities (Scotland) Act of 1889. Without Mr Stewart's contribution this book may be likened to a play without a third act; but it is hoped that the present instalment will not only instruct the historically minded but also entertain anyone who, for whatever reason, takes an interest in the history of the University.

In writing this book I owe most to Miss Helen Armet, Keeper of the Burgh Records, and Mr C. P. Finlayson, MA, Keeper of Manuscripts in the University Library, who directed me to the original sources in their custody and helped me to assess their value. Mr Finlayson has also substantially widened and improved the choice of illustrations, which add so much to the text. I wish also to place on record my indebtedness to Mr R. G. Cant, who read the whole of the typescript and made many valuable suggestions for its correction and improvement, and to Professor Gordon Donaldson, whose scholarship saved me from error in the first chapter where I am a stranger in an unfamiliar century. The errors that remain are my own. Amongst other friends who have helped in various ways are Dr Neil Campbell, Dr Annie Dunlop, Dr J. C. Corson, Dr Ian B. Cowan, Dr J. V. Compton, Sir John Clerk, Bt. of Penicuik, Mr John Chiene, CA, Dr Douglas Guthrie, Mr I. H. Macdonald, WS, Mr Stuart Maxwell, Dr David

C. Simpson, Mr Basil Skinner, and Mr R. Maxwell Young, ssc. I owe much to the chiefs and staffs of the University Library, National Library of Scotland, Edinburgh Public Library, and Scottish Record Office and would ask them to excuse the informality of this *omnibus* expression of thanks for their multifarious and diverse contributions to the making of this book. Sir John Summerson made both pleasant and profitable my visit to the Soane Museum to examine the plans for Adam's Old College; and the Clerk to the George Heriot's Trust gave me access to their early records relating to University bursaries. The Secretary of the Merchant Company was kind enough to permit me to examine original drawings of the University buildings.

Finally, I may be allowed to mention that its production became almost a family affair. As always the help afforded by my wife (Barbara Mary Scott, MA (Edin.) 1922) was by no means confined to reading successive typescripts and proofs, commenting on them with care and discrimination and compiling the index. My elder daughter (Hazel Horn, MA (Edin.) 1958) brought to my attention some documents which might otherwise have escaped notice, and helped me to read them. My son-in-law (Walter Cairns, MUS BAC (Edin.) 1952) guided me, with equal firmness and discretion, through the maze that lies between a typescript, no matter how carefully revised, and the printed word. I can only hope that those who buy the book will find it half as attractive to read as it is to look at in the bookseller's shop.

D. B. HORN

Edinburgh, 18 April 1966

Contents

(5)

The Transition to the Modern University, 1858–1889

Illustrations

DEDICATED
WITHOUT THEIR PERMISSION
TO THE OLDER HISTORIANS
OF THE UNIVERSITY

Thomas Craufurd

AND

Andrew Dalzel

WITHOUT WHOSE HELP
THIS BOOK COULD NOT
HAVE BEEN WRITTEN

Origins and Early Days
of the College
1556 – 1700

ORIGINS

THE COLLEGE of Edinburgh traditionally dates its foundation from the grant of a royal charter by King James VI to the town council of Edinburgh in 1582. Earlier Scottish universities had all received the blessing of the Pope as well as of the King of Scots, and the local bishop contributed substantially to the endowment of the new institution and became its chancellor. Although the royal charter of 1582 was indispensable, it was merely the culmination of a long struggle to provide for university education at Edinburgh.

The medieval universities of Scotland had had occasional periods of prosperity and had produced some outstanding scholars and administrators, although the ablest of their pupils almost invariably continued their education abroad, and there are few indications that they had ever been able to attract foreign scholars. By the first half of the sixteenth century all three were declining, if not actually moribund. In the opinion of its own rector St Andrews had almost

1. Mary of Guise, painted in 1558 and attributed to Corneille de Lyon.

perished and was not worthy to be called a university. Glasgow and Aberdeen were in even worse case. The number of students at Glasgow showed a very dangerous decline before the Reformation and when Queen Mary visited the town in 1563 she saw 'the decay of ane universitie' rather than 'ane establisst foundatioun'. And although Aberdeen is believed to have been the leading Scottish university in the early sixteenth century, yet, when it was visited by its rector in 1549, important officials were absent without leave from the college and there were practically no Arts students except the thirteen bursars. Again, in 1562, if we may accept the statement of the English ambassador to Scotland, it had decayed to such an extent that it had only fifteen or sixteen scholars. The decay of scholarship and the lack of 'cunning' and learned men had become commonplace long before the Reformation changed the nature of, and aggravated, the problem.

It is true that Archbishop Hamilton was trying energetically and not without some success to infuse new life into the metropolitan university of St Andrews, and that one provincial council of the Scottish Church after another made ordinances intended to improve the education of the clergy. The magnitude and significance of the problem was evident to contemporaries, and in 1556, before the Scottish Reformation had been effected, the administration of Mary of Guise had appointed two eminent scholars, Alexander Sym and Edward Henderson, to lecture publicly in Edinburgh on civil and canon law, Greek, and other sciences. Each scholar was to receive £100 (Scots) directly out of the Treasury for his services, a sum considerably in excess of the normal salaries payable to regents at the Scottish universities. The town council fitted up the Magdalen Chapel in the Cowgate to enable the professors to give their lectures there during the session 1556–7. Since payments were made to them out of the Treasury for two or three years we may reasonably assume that some lectures were actually given; but it is impossible to resist the conclusion that this first College of Edinburgh disappeared in the tumult of the Reformation, if not earlier. It bore a remarkable resemblance to the Collège de France, founded at Paris by Francis I a few years earlier.

Some of the Reformers must have been aware of Mary of Guise's experiment, although there is no specific reference to it in the First Book of Discipline which sets out their ideas on education. They regarded the three existing universities as sufficient for the national needs and made no suggestion that a fourth university, located at Edinburgh or elsewhere, was either necessary or desirable. They did however propose to establish in every notable town a college in which the Arts, at least Logic and Rhetoric, together with the tongues Latin, Greek, and possibly Hebrew, would be read by sufficient masters. Had the First Book of Discipline been translated into fact in 1560 such a college would certainly have been established at Edinburgh; but there was no chance that the 'devout imaginations' of the Reformers, which included the establishment of a national system of education from the primary school to post-graduate colleges, would be realised in sixteenth-century Scotland.

In the Canongate 1814

Chapel & Hospital of St. Mary Magdalene.

2. The Magdalen Chapel where University lectures were first given in Edinburgh, 1556–7; etching by Paterson, 1816.

Nevertheless their ideas, after a long struggle with the indifference of Mary Queen of Scots and the self-interested opposition of James VI's courtiers and advisers, led to the establishment of the University of Edinburgh. Under the leadership of the Edinburgh ministers, the town council finally secured royal sanction, a site for the College, and even a modest grant-in-aid out of the revenues of the old Church.

Supremacy of Redson over Anger & all passions. J am so weel satisfied with this days exercise that J will be God-Father to the Colledge of Edinburgh and haue it called The Col--ledge of King Iames; for after the foundation of it had been stopped for sundry years in my minority, so shoon as J came to any knowledge J zealously held hand to it and caused it to be Established, And altho J see many looke upon it with Ane evill eye, yet J will haue them to know that haueing given it This Name I haue espoused its querrell.

3. Thomas Craufurd records James VI's decision to support the University in 1617; from a transcript of Craufurd's *History of the University of Edinburgh, 1580–1646*, made in 1673 by William Henderson, Librarian to the University.

The council were lucky to obtain also control of a part of a legacy left by Robert Reid, Bishop of Orkney, in 1558 to establish a College of Law on the south side of Edinburgh.

The Tounis College, as it soon came to be called, was intended to carry out the academic ideals of Calvin in the production of good Christians who would also be intelligent and responsible citizens. But it was to be no mere College of the Liberal Arts; it was expressly authorised to establish all the higher faculties. On the other hand the charter of 1582 made no mention whatever of the power to grant degrees. Arts degrees were in practice given from the beginning; but it was not until the Act of 1621 that the legal basis of Edinburgh degrees was placed beyond cavil.

This Act of the Scottish Parliament is often regarded as the equivalent of the God-bairn gift which James VI, on his visit to Scotland in 1617, is said to have promised the masters of the College. While he was in Edinburgh, James VI was too busy to visit the College, but later in the summer he summoned the masters to Stirling where they conducted in the King's presence an elaborate debate, while James behaved himself like an academic clown and made atrocious puns on the masters' surnames. Henceforth the College of Edinburgh, he decided, should be known in all time coming as King James's College. The town council had no choice but to obey, although they continued also to use the older title. To this day the inscription over the main entrance to the Old Quadrangle describes the institution in occupation of the building as James the Sixth's Academy. The historians of the University have held and no doubt will continue to hold very different views on the true significance of the Act of 1621; but it was certainly intended to place King James's College on a level in all respects with the older universities of Scotland. This it effectively did and we need not enquire further into its significance.*

THE SIXTEENTH-CENTURY COLLEGE

Actual instruction in the College began in 1583 in charge of a young St Andrews graduate, Robert Rollock, but many would-be students were found to be insufficiently acquainted with Latin to understand his lectures. Another young man, Duncan Nairne, a Glasgow graduate, was therefore appointed to instruct them in Latin so that they could pass a kind of preliminary examination and begin a degree course in the following year. From the very beginning the new venture was a success. Within a few years Edinburgh could–and did–boast that it had more students than any of the older universities had or ever had had. These students followed a regular four-year course in Arts and as soon as the first class had qualified as Masters of Arts a considerable number of them then studied Divinity for a further period. In Arts they were taught not by specialist professors, as the leading university reformers of the sixteenth century had demanded, but by regents, each of whom taught all the subjects in the curriculum, beginning with Greek in the first year and proceeding in later years through the various branches of Philosophy. Each Arts student had the same teacher for the whole of his course, but regents in the early days of the College usually contrived to find better jobs for themselves after two or three years and the instruction of their

---

* Readers who are interested in the origins of the University of Edinburgh may care to refer to two articles by the present writer in the *University of Edinburgh Journal* for the spring and autumn terms, 1966.

4. Principal Robert Rollock; detail from an anonymous painting of 1599.

students had to be taken over by a successor. Rollock was appointed first principal and then specialised in teaching divinity. His staff consisted of four philosophy regents and one regent of humanity whose status and functions were clearly inferior to those of his colleagues.

The College classes were at first held in a house built by James Hamilton, second Earl of Arran, often known by his French title as Duke of Châtelherault, shortly after 1554 on part of the site which the town council had hoped to secure for the College in 1562 and had actually obtained twenty years later. The site was partly occupied with other buildings, including the ruined Collegiate Church of St Mary in the Fields, popularly known as the Kirk o' Field, and the lodgings of its canons and other officials. In one of these Darnley was living at the time of his murder a few years before the establishment of the Tounis College. There is also an ancient tradition countenanced by Principal Robertson that the house occupied by the eighteenth-century principals of the University, if indeed it was not the actual house of the sixteenth-century Provosts of the Collegiate Church, at least stood on its site.

While it is possible that other buildings already on the site may have been used for academic purposes, the evidence suggests that the Duke of Châtelherault's large and commodious mansion, which was extensively adapted by the town council for the purpose, provided for the first generations of students all the classrooms that were required. Indeed most classes down to the early eighteenth century continued to meet in this building, which came to be known as the duke's lodging or Hamilton House. Since the town council in the early days of the College still had in view a residential college, they were bound to make some provision for student bedchambers. They therefore devoted to this purpose the diminished legacy which they received about this time from the estate of Robert Reid, Bishop of Orkney. Fourteen bedchambers, later referred to in the College records as the old or Reid Chambers, were built to the east of the duke's lodging and arrangements were made to rent them to the students, at a charge of £2 each for the session, if two students shared a bed. Any student who required a bed to himself must pay £4. The rents would be used to furnish the chambers with 'treyne beds, buirdis, and skelffis'. Children of Edinburgh burgesses would be exempt from payment of rent, but would be required 'to sett up their beds, buirdis, and skelffis upoun their own proper chairgis'.

Although dire penalties were invoked in the early laws of the

College against students who did not wear gowns in the day time and lie nightly in the College, it is certain that the concourse of students was so great that the bedchambers provided by the town council could not house all those who enrolled as students. Even the fourteen Reid Chambers were not ready for occupation when the first batch of students were enrolled. But the clearest proof that from its earliest days the College was not in fact residential is that no steward can be found on the lists of College officials and no 'common table' for teachers and students was ever established.

No doubt expense and lack of accommodation explain the absence of what was usually regarded until the nineteenth century as an essential need for all colleges; but it is worth remembering that the ideas of the Scottish reformers, notably as stated in the First Book of Discipline, included the belief that the youthhead should be nourished and brought up in virtue 'in presence of their friends'. Here 'friends' must be used in the ancient Scots meaning, which even now survives in the Scots vernacular, of relations. In other words students should not be removed from their families and immured in a residential college. That this idea survived well into the seventeenth century at Edinburgh is proved by the attitude of a section of the town council to the provision by private benefactors of student chambers.

THE SEVENTEENTH-CENTURY COLLEGE

The College of Edinburgh changed little in basic structure during this century. In 1700 it was still essentially an Arts college with a Divinity school attached. To judge by the list of private benefactions, the citizens of Edinburgh were proud of their College and considered its chief need to be more specialised instruction in Divinity. This was achieved in the course of the century by the creation of Chairs of Divinity, Oriental Languages, and Ecclesiastical History. By this time too there was a Chair of Mathematics, occupied in succession by three members of the famous professorial family of Gregory. Occasional attempts had been made to extend the instruction offered by the College to include Law and Medicine; and regular teaching in Medicine was just beginning at the end of the seventeenth century.

The increase in the number of students and the growing pride of the town council in their College produced dissatisfaction with the original makeshift building. In particular, Hamilton House had no room large enough for the daily meetings of the whole College for

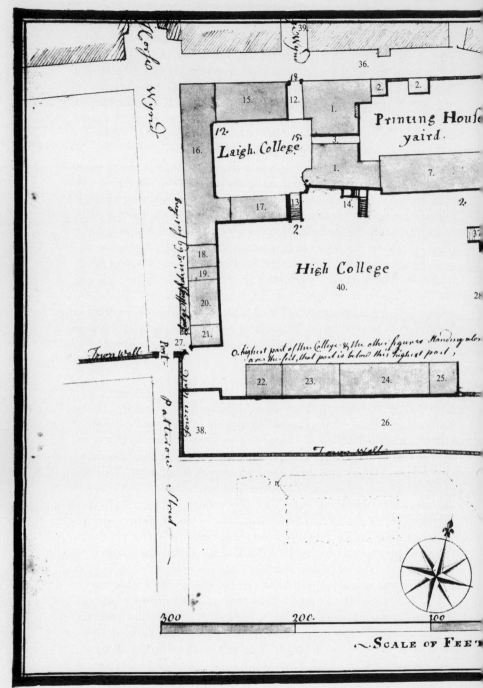

The text visible within the image:

Cowfo Wynd

39

36.

Printing House yaird.

2. 2.

18

15. 12.

1.

12. 15.

Laigh College

16

3.

1. 7.

17. 13.

14. 2.

2' 37

High College

18. 40.

19.

28

20. 0. highest part of the College & the other figures standing along are the feit, that part is below this highest part,

21.

27 22. 23. 24. 25.

Town Wall Port-

26.

38.

Town Wall

300. 200. 100.

SCALE OF FEET

5. The buildings of the Tounis College as shown on John Laurie's plan of 1767. (For key to printed numbers see p. 12).

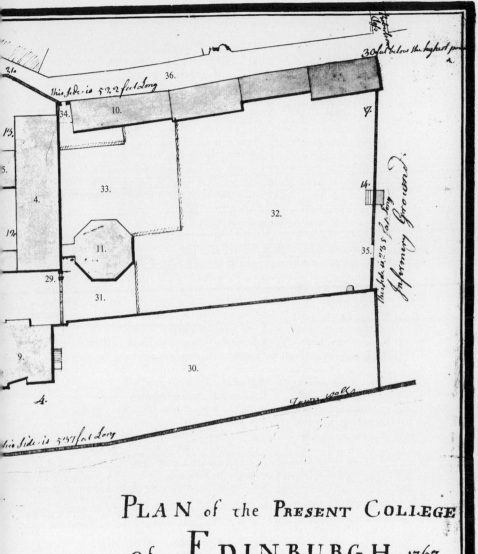

PLAN of the PRESENT COLLEGE of EDINBURGH. 1767.

by John Laurie

Content is { 138312. Sq feet
15368. Sq yards } and { 4 : R ... poles
3 : 0 ... 28 English
4 : R ... Sq
2 : 2 ... 49 Scots }

1. Hamilton House or the Duke's Lodging. As well as classrooms there was room here for a few student chambers (three in 1625).
2. Site of Old or Reid Chambers.
3. Laigh Transe, linking Laigh College with Printing House yaird.
4. The 1617 Building: Great Hall below, Library above when completed. Subsequent uses varied. The garret above was used mainly by the University printers in the early eighteenth century.
5. Jamb of 1617 Building originally occupied as two student chambers.
6. Heich Transe from High College to Printing House yaird.
7. The 1642 Library building, often called the New Library. One storey to the south, but as seen from Printing House yaird, it had 'an arched sunk storey and principal floor with a leaden roof' (Dalzel's *History*).
8. Forecourt of 1617 Building.
9. Principal's house.
10. The house of the professor of Divinity. The original house bought in 1642 for the professor of Divinity stood in High School Yards. It was sold in 1656 to the College of Surgeons and the purchase price applied to building a house in the University precinct.
11. New Anatomy theatre.
12. Main entrance, with Jossie's chamber above, built 1636–7 but 'rowinous' by 1690, and (after 1700) replaced by Burnet's tower.
13. Jossie's steps, built *c.* 1640 to improve access to High College.
14. Outside staircase built by Jossie *c.* 1640 giving access to classrooms in Hamilton House: this was built to avoid disturbances when classes were using the staircase inside Hamilton House.
15–21. Student chambers built between 1625 and 1660.
22–25. Student chambers built in the Restoration period (1660–85).
26. Archery butts 1673.
27. Side entrance from Potterow described in 1658 as 'the new back gate'.
28, 29. Gates providing access through the old site or garden of the Wishart/Pillans house to the new Anatomy theatre 1764.
30. Private garden attached to principal's house.
31. Garden of Wishart/Pillans house or possibly part of the garden of the professor of Divinity.
32. College garden with fruit and ornamental trees and laid out in trim walks in the later seventeenth century.
33. Garden attached to the house of the professor of Divinity.
34. Entrance to the house of the professor of Divinity from Jamaica Lane.
35. Access to grounds of Royal Infirmary.
36. Jamaica Lane.
37. Flight of steps giving access to the forecourt of the 1617 Building.
38. Approximate site of latrines after 1628–9.
39. College Wynd.
40. High College: 'rid of the rubbish of the Old Kirk of Field and cast into three level walks' (1628–9; Craufurd's *History*).

6. Commemorative inscription placed by the Town Council on the 1617 Building, now built into the wall of the Court Room vestibule.

prayers, while the annual laureations had to be held in one or other of the town churches. A two-storey building, over one hundred feet in length and about thirty feet broad, was therefore erected on a site to the south-east of Hamilton House in the years after 1616. The lower floor of the new building was used as a common hall; the upper floor, originally intended to be the refectory or dining hall, served as the Library of the College. It bore the inscription *Senatus Populusque Edinburgensis has aedes Christo et Musis extruendas curarunt* and gave great satisfaction to the College authorities at the time, who referred to it, at the graduation of 1620, as *speciosas et spatiosas aedes*.

Yet only twenty years later Hamilton House and the 1617 building were judged inadequate and the most important period of building—prior to Adam—in the history of the College began. Credit for this should perhaps be shared by John Jossie, one of the town councillors and subsequently College treasurer, and the covenanting rector, Alexander Henderson. It was Jossie who built what was to be for over 150 years the main entrance to the College. This was on the north side of the present Old Quadrangle, immediately adjoining the duke's lodging, on the west, and facing College Wynd, a steep narrow lane running down to the Cowgate. This westward extension of the College buildings revealed 'some baggage thatched houses' which not only detracted from the dignity of the new entrance, but were believed to house ladies whose society was unsuitable for students. These houses were purchased and in 1638 a wall was erected around them running west till it reached Horse Wynd, at the north-west corner of the present Old Quadrangle, and then south. The old houses were then pulled down.

A few years later an entirely new Library building was erected to link the southern wing of the duke's lodging with the west wing projecting from the 1617 Library and common hall. The new Library, which was built in the years after 1642, appeared as a single storey from the south, as seen in Gordon of Rothiemay's plan of Edinburgh; but from the north, where the ground was lower, an arched sunk storey, supported on pillars carried forward into the old lower court of the College, was seen below the main storey.

Concurrently with these developments went the provision of student chambers. These were built mainly at the expense of private benefactors and were not intended to provide sleeping accommodation, but merely studies to which students could retire between classes and do some reading on their own. They correspond exactly to the reading rooms which are now an integral part of library provision for the needs of twentieth-century students. A benefactor who provided money to build these chambers usually stipulated that he and his descendants should name the students who, during their course at Edinburgh, were to have the use of the studies. If there was no preferential candidate, the town council let the chambers to students who were prepared to pay a fixed annual charge which varied according to the accommodation provided.

The earliest of these were the fourteen old chambers to the east of the duke's lodging, facing on the old lower court, which the town council had built out of Reid's diminished legacy in the sixteenth century. No trace of them can be found when lists of chambers appear in the city records towards the end of the seventeenth century. Either they had become ruinous—a not infrequent occurrence with College buildings in the seventeenth century—or they were being used as

---

7. The College, facing west. On the left are the Teviot Chambers separated by the 'new back gate' from (centre) another row of student chambers and the Adam Department of Anatomy. On the extreme right is the 1642 Library reconstructed in 1767 (see Figure 8); from *Edinburgh in the Olden Time*, 1880.

classrooms. But new chambers were continually being built by pious benefactors of the College. When Jossie extended the College precinct to the west and built the external wall of 1638 the north and west sides of the new lower court were soon completely occupied by student chambers. In addition to these north and west ranges of chambers, a short wing of similar rooms projected eastwards towards the duke's lodging from the west range and formed a dividing line between the new lower court to the north and the great or higher court to the south. Access to the higher court was at first obtained only from the new lower court by means of Jossie's steps; but later a new entrance was constructed on the west side, approximately on the line of the present back entry to the Old Quadrangle.

In the 1650s more chambers were built to the west of the great court; the principal's house, at the south-east corner of the great court, was reconstructed; and the house of the professor of Divinity was built to the east of the old lower court. In the Restoration period a long range of student chambers, most of them paid for from a bequest by a former student of the College, the Earl of Teviot, were erected on the south side of the great court. Shortly afterwards student chambers became an anachronism. No more were built and the benefactors who would formerly have made bequests and gifts to build these chambers now founded bursaries. An appreciable proportion of student chambers built in the seventeenth century are described in a return of 1690 as 'waste' or 'ruinous': those that continued in use were either transformed into classrooms, annexed by the professors for their own use, or let by the town council to a motley crew of tenants. Early in the eighteenth century a high steeple, crowning a narrow five-storeyed tower, was built over the main entrance. This was Burnet's steeple, so called because built out of funds given to the College by Thomas Burnet. Originally intended as a bell-tower, it was not in fact used for this purpose; the old College bell continued to hang in an older bell-tower on a site which cannot be identified with certainty.

8. The High College, facing north. Student chambers, on the left, adjoin a
   central gap where Jossie's steps provide access from the Laigh College
   in the background. Burnet's steeple is behind the 1642 Library (shown
   prior to its reconstruction). On the extreme right is the 1617 Building
   (see Figure 28); from *Edinburgh in the Olden Time*, 1880. Hamilton House,
   which should appear between Jossie's steps and the 1642 Library,
   has for some unknown reason been omitted from this drawing.

The town council had begun in 1583 with a makeshift building, Hamilton House, and although they spent in the next 200 years substantial sums on new buildings, specifically designed to serve academic purposes, no serious attempt had as yet been made to harmonise and regularise the appearance of the buildings. While there were three quadrangles, only one, the new lower court, was completely surrounded by buildings. None of the quadrangles had been accurately levelled; and although causeways had been laid between the most popular places of resort and, in addition to Jossie's steps, there were at least two transes or passages – known as the Heich Transe and the Laich Transe* – the quadrangles were regularly'encumbered with rubbish and the ground must, in bad weather, have been churned into a quagmire.

English visitors nearly always wrote contemptuously of the buildings which were sometimes contrasted with the 'neat college' at Glasgow. John Ray, the naturalist, was reminded by the Edinburgh buildings of Caius College, Cambridge, while he thought the college at Glasgow not inferior to Wadham or All Souls at Oxford. In self-defence Principal Robertson, in showing round tourists of the calibre of Dr Johnson, was prone to anticipate criticism by telling them the story of a foreign Jesuit who, in performing the same service for visitors to his college, described the buildings as *'Hae miseriae nostrae'*. The features of the College which impressed visitors favourably were the College Library and the miscellaneous collection of curiosities housed in the Common Hall – and of course the very extensive grounds to the east of the College. The original Kirk o' Field site had been considerably extended in this direction and, in the second half of the seventeenth century, this ground had been levelled, planted with fruit and ornamental trees, and laid out in trim walks. Not only did the principal and the professor of Divinity have their own private gardens, but there was also a College garden, where the professors and students recreated themselves after an exhausting day in the classrooms.

While the principal and the professor of Divinity had established by the mid-seventeenth century a right to an official residence in the College precinct, the other teachers had no such claim. Gradually a number of them succeeded by persistent pressure in securing suites of rooms in College for themselves and a few managed to acquire fully

---

* See Figure 5.

equipped houses. When the old buildings were pulled down in 1790, the professor of Divinity lived at the north-east corner of the precinct and the professors of Hebrew and Greek at the north-west corner. These professorial encroachments were usually effected by the occupation of chambers originally intended for students and therefore diminished the revenue derived by the town council from letting such rooms. It should be added that the town council also encroached on the accommodation available for students by granting College rooms rent free to College officials, such as the janitor and gardener, or by setting them in tack (lease) to persons who had no right to accommodation in the College but who could afford to pay an economic rent.

TOWN-COUNCIL CONTROL AND FINANCE

The government of the College was vested in the town council who came to talk of themselves as the patrons. At first the enrolment of students was entrusted to the bailies and the council laid down in minute detail rules for the conduct of teachers and students. A body such as the town council had, however, to delegate authority in the day-to-day conduct of the College. Much was soon left to the principal, and the town council experimented with the office of rector, the lack of which office was felt to take away from the dignity of the College in comparison with other universities. In their view the essential function of the rector was not to defend academic privileges but to act as the eye of the town council. As soon as the council developed other means of inspecting the College, the office of rector disappeared for two centuries from the College annals.

In 1665, the council tried another experiment, when they decided that the Lord Provost in all time coming should be chancellor and made good this appointment against the claims to the office of the Restoration Bishop of Edinburgh. In later seventeenth-century practice, however, the College council, which included a large representation of the town council along with the ministers of Edinburgh and leading members of the College staff, usually made recommendations on College business to the town council, which thus retained the final decision. In the early eighteenth century the College council was replaced by a committee of the town council headed by one of the bailies, known as the College bailie. As the College grew in size and reputation, and the transient regents were replaced by eminent specialist professors with a European reputation, occasional conflict

9. James VI; an engraving which appears opposite the title-page of
The Muses' Welcome, a eulogistic collection addressed to James
on the occasion of his visit to Scotland in 1617.

between the patrons and the teaching staff was probably inevitable.
It culminated in the thirty-year war between the Senate and the
town council in the first half of the nineteenth century.

Control of the purse strings until the passing of the Universities
(Scotland) Act of 1858 always rested with the town council. There
were three main sources of College revenue: (1) kirk annuals or
teinds *(anglice tithes)*; (2) mortcloth dues; and (3) benefactions.
Certain revenues belonging to the pre-Reformation Church had been

given by Mary Queen of Scots to the town of Edinburgh and James VI had authorised the town to apply, at their discretion, part of these revenues to the upkeep of the College. He had shortly afterwards given the corporation the teinds of Currie to supplement these other revenues. A few years later the Presbytery of Edinburgh had given a substantial sum of money towards the upkeep of the College on condition that the corporation set aside for the same purpose the sums it received from mortcloth dues. The town council enjoyed a monopoly of supplying velvet palls for use at funerals within the town and enforced this rigidly against any would-be competitors. Important and wealthy mourners, outside of the city boundaries, also often made use of this service, and the profits which resulted were applied for centuries to the cost of running the College. Private benefactors also gave money to the council to endow the College or, more frequently, for specific purposes which they had at heart, such as the foundation and further endowment of the Chair of Divinity.

Had the town council applied these sums to the purchase of land within or around the city, the University of Edinburgh would now be far richer than Heriot's Trust and the Merchant Company put together. Unfortunately, their finances were always in a muddle and in the early years of the College they made no distinction between College and town revenues and property. When in 1640 they did try to separate the two accounts they reckoned that they had received £14,070 Scots from College benefactors and decided to pay to the College interest on it at current rates in all time coming. The annual charge thus received speedily diminished as rates of interest fell. Also with continual inflation the real value of the fixed annual revenue steadily declined. As new benefactions were received after 1640 the corporation merely increased proportionately the mythical sum upon which they paid interest to the College.

It is fair to add that since the revenue from all sources hardly ever covered the council's expenditure on the College, the deficit had to be made up out of the council's other funds. Moreover most benefactors tied up their gifts to some specific purpose, such as the endowment of a particular Chair, the foundation of a bursary, to which the founder and his descendants would have in perpetuity a right of nomination, or the building of one or more student chambers in the College. As late as the Revolution of 1688 the whole revenues of the College from Currie teinds, mortcloth dues, the interest on benefactions paid by the corporation to the College, and the rents collected from the occupiers of College rooms, did not exceed £700 sterling. Fifty years earlier the whole revenues of the University of Glasgow amounted to £368 sterling.*

On the expenditure side of the College accounts much the largest item was salaries of teaching staff. The principal's salary was so small that for long he could only make ends meet by pluralism: he served usually as one of the town's ministers or at least discharged some of the duties attached to this office. Later still he was often given the sinecure office of dean of the chapel royal. The salaries of the professors varied considerably, but the professors, like the principal, often supplemented their modest salaries by taking other jobs. The salaries of the regents were tiny, but they collected substantial sums from each pupil at the beginning of the session and, when it was their turn to conduct the laureation ceremony at the end of each four years' course, they received a gratuity from each graduand. The amount of this in the later seventeenth century was individually assessed by two graduands chosen by their fellows and endowed with the titles of President and Quaestor. Poor students were, however, exempted from payments to regents. Thomas Boston calculated that his three years' course in Arts (1691–4) cost him in fees to regents, College dues, and his own maintenance during the sessions, £10 14s. 7⅔d. sterling for the three years. He added that he had 'lived meanly and perhaps more so than was needful or reasonable'.

Towards the end of the seventeenth century the salaries paid in cash by the town council to the teaching and administrative staff of the College amounted in the aggregate to between £450 and £550 sterling *per annum*. Since the establishment by this time included a principal, eight professors or regents, and a librarian, it will be obvious that none of these officials was overpaid. Substantial sums in the aggregate, amounting to about £200 sterling before the institution of William III's bursaries, were doled out in pitifully small sums to a large number of College bursars. Some of these were for Arts students, others were intended to enable Arts graduates to continue their studies in the Faculty of Divinity. Heriot's Hospital, under their statutes, awarded annually several such bursaries to their boys; and a substantial part of William III's grant was, for a time, used to increase the number of bursaries in Divinity. The third main item on the discharge side of the accounts was expenditure on College build-

---

* James Coutts, *History of the University of Glasgow*, p. 97.

ings. Since this varied greatly from year to year no annual figure has meaning.

THE LAWS AND ROUTINE OF THE COLLEGE: 1583–1700

In the early days lectures began at six o'clock in winter and five in summer. Before this the bursars were expected to 'paidell' or clean the floors and passages, while one of them had to ring the bell to summon the other students to work. The regents read their lectures at dictation speed, hence lectures were often called 'dictates'. After lecturing, they went over the same ground again several times, firing a continual stream of questions, mixed with exhortation and abuse, at their students until they were satisfied that the lesson had been thoroughly grasped by all. In addition to these meetings in the private schools, public lectures were given by the professors, and the principal frequently preached and lectured to the whole College. In winter all students were marched to the playing fields on the Burgh muir 'benorth the gallowis' to disport themselves under the watchful eyes of the regents between the hours of two and four. In summer this treat was postponed until later in the day. Summer and winter, as soon as the students returned to the College, the monotonous round of lectures, tutorials, and oral examinations was resumed, and continued, until late in the evening. Much time was devoted also to declamations and discussions; and, after careful preparation, each class was expected to show its prowess before the whole College. At other times the senior classes conducted public debates with each other on topics proposed by the regents. Such public exhibitions of dialectical skill often took place on Saturdays.

Sundays were devoted mainly to religious exercises. There was no College chapel; but the town council arranged for the regents and students to attend divine service and sit together in a loft in one of the town churches. This meant attendance morning and afternoon. When this rigid system was breaking down towards the end of the seventeenth century, a visitor noted that College discipline was less strict at Edinburgh than at Glasgow because at Edinburgh by this time students were required to attend only the morning service. On returning to the College, students went to their own class rooms where they were examined on the sermons, taught the catechisms, and otherwise instructed in their religious duties. The object of the Scottish universities in this period was to inculcate piety and good

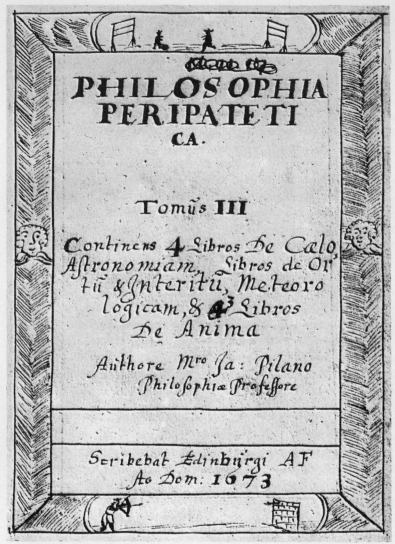

PHILOSOPHIA
PERIPATETI
CA.

Tomũs III

Continens 4 Libros De Cælo,
Astronomiam, Libros de Or
tũ & Interitũ, Meteoro
logicam, & 3 Libros
De Anima

Authore Mro Ja: Pilano
Philosophiæ Professore

Scribebat Edinburgi AF
Ao Dom: 1673

10. Title-page from Archibald Flint's autograph notes of one of Regent
Pillans' courses of lectures, with two decorative drawings of students
engaged in sporting activities. These notes illustrate the elaborate care
taken by many students in recording lectures.

learning and there is no doubt that contemporaries put piety first. Until the Restoration period each regent carried a staff and one of the recognised duties of the principal was the public chastisement of unruly pupils.

Any break in this monotonous existence must have been looked forward to and we need not be surprised to find the town council prohibiting students from attending funerals, except those of lords of session, 'prime advocates' or magistrates of the city. In the earliest days of the College the students were allowed only a month's vacation in the year, usually the month of August, but this was gradually extended and about a week's break was also allowed between Christmas and the New Year. Even terminal examinations might have been a welcome change from monotony but they were unknown. A regent who did not examine a substantial proportion of his students every day was failing to discharge the duties of his office – and might himself be discharged. Several student notebooks of this early period are preserved in the University Library. Not only do they enable us to determine the way in which the regent handled his subject; they sometimes also show scribblings and drawings made by individual students while sitting in the classroom. One of these, reproduced on page 26, depicts the costume worn by regents; another gives a glimpse of one of the steeples which adorned the College as seen presumably from the classroom window. The most important formal examinations took place at the beginning – not the end – of each session and lasted for some weeks until the principal and regents had satisfied themselves that the individual student had mastered the work of the previous year sufficiently to enable him to cope with the next year's course.

At last, after nearly four years of grind, came the day of manumission and release from tutelage. 'All cloathed in black gowns after the fashion of their professor', the successful magistrands, who had been carefully coached for weeks beforehand in their parts, paraded in one of the town's churches or in their own common hall. The town's ministers were there in force, accompanied not only by the Provost, bailies, and members of the council, but by a distinguished gathering which included lords of session and prime advocates and even one or two of the great officers of state. The regent whose students were to be laureated had prepared a long list of theses, ethical, philosophical, mathematical, and so on, which had been printed with the names of the graduands attached.

11. Decorated capital letters from Archibald Flint's notes of Pillans'
lectures, showing the costume worn by seventeenth-century regents,
and a college steeple.

By previous searching examination the graduands had been
arranged in a rough order of merit. First came the '*exortes* before all
the circles', then 'some in the first circle; some annexed thereto; some
in the second circle; the remainder in a line, whose names are
thought fittest to be spared in public calling upon them'. Sometimes
harangues were delivered in Latin, Greek, and Hebrew by the best
students, some of whom were called to defend, others to attack the
theses. Some of the mathematical theses seem to have been demonstrated on the blackboard by students who had specialised in this branch
of knowledge. A magistrand who impressed the distinguished audience
favourably by his share in the harangues and disputations had laid
the foundation of his career in church or state. It is worth labouring
the point that the pristine Arts degree of the University of Edinburgh
was not what we call now an ordinary or pass degree, but was
awarded after highly competitive examination over a wide field of
knowledge. The nearest equivalent to it in the twentieth century
would be the examinations for the administrative grade of the Civil
Service before these were reduced in scope after the First World War.
    The laureation ceremonies described in the preceding paragraph

12. The oldest extant MA diploma, with signatures of principal, professors, and regents, and showing the use of one of the town's seals.

were undoubtedly a much simplified version of the elaborate medieval examination procedures and techniques which were in use in the
late-medieval Scots universities. These have recently been examined
by Dr Annie Dunlop with special reference to St Andrews,* where
'circling' of licentiates was practised in the first half of the sixteenth
century and seems to have continued in use until the end of the
seventeenth. In 1695 two of the St Andrews colleges claimed that
their university was the only one in Scotland to retain this practice.
At Edinburgh 'circling' in its full rigour had fallen out of use earlier.
The most important difference between seventeenth-century and
late-medieval examination techniques was the introduction of the
group or class thesis. This presumably had its late-medieval origins
in the St Andrews practice of examining candidates for the licentiate
in groups and then placing them in an order of merit which took
account of other factors than intellectual attainment. The early
abandonment of 'circling' at Edinburgh was certainly due in part to
the refusal of the College authorities to award first-class degrees to
the doltish sons of influential parents. The modified form of 'circling'
in vogue at Edinburgh in the later seventeenth century, in conjunction with a group thesis, had the advantage that such well-connected
young men could be awarded degrees without exposing them to the
perils of a public oral examination conducted in a language in which
they were unlikely to be fluent.

The town council did its best to conduct laureations with dignity
and decorum. The hall in which the ceremony was to take place was
fitted up with benches; carpets were provided for the distinguished
guests and soldiers were employed, presumably as door-keepers.
Hour glasses were used to regulate the length of the orations and
disputations.

Although a form of 'circling' and public laureations continued into
the early eighteenth century, the importance attached to them
declined in the second half of the seventeenth century. This was
partly due to politico-ecclesiastical factions. Presbyterian students,
who had successfully completed the four years' course, refused to take
oaths of allegiance to the episcopalian regime and could not therefore be laureated. Similarly after the Revolution of 1688 the Episcopalians usually declined to comply with the formalities required from

---

* *Acta Facultatis Artium Universitatis Sanctiandree 1413-1588*, I, pp. lxxxix–
cxxii.

THESES
PHILOSOPHICAE,
Quas auſpice & propitio Deo
propugnabunt adoleſcentes hoc
ANNO 1617. *Magiſterio
donandi, Edinburgi, in*
æde ſacra Regii Colle-
gii, a.d. Iunii.

PRÆSIDE ANDREA IVNIO.

EDINBVRGI,
Excudebat Andreas Hart, ANNO DOM. 1617.

13. Title-page of a seventeenth-century group thesis dedicated to James VI.

all students before graduation. It appears also that many students
refused, for reasons of their own unconnected with politics, to remain
in Edinburgh during the two or three months' gap between the end
of teaching in the magistrand class and the actual laureation ceremony, nor would they incur the trouble and expense of returning to

the town for the laureation. The regents complained therefore that, since so few students attended, public laureations were no longer sufficiently profitable to the regents nor were they a good advertisement for the College. Somewhat reluctantly the town council accepted these arguments and allowed the regents to conduct private laureations for small groups, or even individual students, at times convenient to themselves. After the early years of the eighteenth century graduation in Arts almost ceased, and although the practice revived slightly in the first half of the nineteenth century, it did not become normal until after the Universities (Scotland) Act of 1858.

STUDENTS AND REGENTS

Edinburgh is lucky in the preservation of records which enable us to state with reasonable accuracy the numbers of its students from its origins to the present day. Craufurd gave a figure of sixteen score as a fair average for the 1630s and the number may have reached nearly 500 in the early years of the Restoration. Dalzel records that the first-year students exceeded 100 for the first time in 1662; but the rate of student wastage in a seventeenth-century college would have given a University Grants Committee hysterics. In many years in the second half of the seventeenth century less than fifty per cent–occasionally less than forty per cent–of the students who entered the College graduated at the normal time. This, of course, was due partly to the ecclesiastical troubles mentioned in the previous paragraph. Therefore an increased number of students at Edinburgh at this time would not be fully reflected in the lists of graduates in the later seventeenth century, although there are in fact a larger number of graduates in the second than in the first half of this century. On the whole it seems doubtful whether Craufurd's figure of 320 was often exceeded until we reach the Hanoverian period. For purposes of comparison it is worth mentioning that in the early seventeenth century Oxford and Cambridge, taken together, were graduating more than 450 men each year and matriculating another 200 to 250 who did not take degrees.* In the late sixteenth and early seventeenth centuries Glasgow seems to have admitted about thirty new students a year, but this had risen by about fifty per cent in the Restoration period. As at Edinburgh, only a fraction of the matriculated students graduated.

---

* W. H. Curtis in *Past and Present*, XXIII, p. 32.

Only five graduates appear on the official register for some years early in the seventeenth century, although this may be due to incomplete recording. By the Restoration twenty or thirty graduates are recorded in most years.* Edinburgh, from the beginning, was graduating about thirty students each year and by the Restoration lists of fifty or sixty graduates are normal.

In the earliest days the great majority of students must have come from the south-east of Scotland and it was long before students were attracted in any number from the Highlands. But even before 1603 a number of foreign students had studied at Edinburgh, mostly French Huguenots and English Presbyterians or Puritans. As the seventeenth century went on the Huguenots, now with adequate educational provision within France, disappeared; but English students increased, especially in the 1640s, and a few Irish students appeared. Eighteen out of the eighty-one graduates of 1697 came from places in the British Isles furth of Scotland.

The town council, early in the eighteenth century, actually supported a private enterprise boarding establishment intended to attract English students to the University. Some of the leading English nonconformists put forward, at this time, ambitious plans to establish a college at Edinburgh, on the Oxford model. Resident students would be coached and carefully supervised. English tutors would preserve the purity of their native language and they would be provided with at least one good meal a day. College tutors would also be available for academic instruction and moral supervision of other English students living in lodgings in the town. Divisions amongst the English nonconformists, fomented apparently by the jealous watchfulness of the University of Glasgow, which was also anxious to tap the English reservoir, prevented the scheme from having any practical results. English nonconformist students continued to resort to Edinburgh in ever increasing numbers in the eighteenth century; but it was probably better for them, and certainly for the University, that they should not be given a privileged status, but should mix on equal terms with their fellow students.

As we have seen, Edinburgh students in the early seventeenth century can have had little spare time during the week. But although the old statutes were reissued from time to time with little change, it is clear from the enquiries of the 1690 Commission on the Scottish

---

* *Munimenta alme Universitatis Glasguensis* (Glasgow 1854) II, pp. 1–161.

Universities that these archaic rules were more honoured in the breach than in the observance. Regents lay in bed on Sunday mornings instead of marshalling their pupils to church; and it was credibly reported of the professor of Mathematics that he went with his pupils on the first Sunday in term and then was seen no more in the College loft until the first Sunday of the following session. Drunkenness and brawling were also imputed to the regents, some of whom hounded on their pupils to attack other classes in the playing fields and elsewhere. One regent assaulted a pupil so severely with his wand of office that henceforth the carrying of staffs was prohibited. Corporal punishment was already on its way out and its place was taken by an elaborate system of fines with, in reserve, the ultimate punishment of extrusion from the College at the hands of the janitor. The decline in moral standards, if not in academic achievement, was due partly to a change in the regents. Earlier they had been young men anxious to secure a patron who would provide them with a parish; now they were often scions of landed families or sons of wealthy merchants who resented any attempt either to impose restrictions on them or curb their passions.

The quarrelsomeness and violence of the regents were matched by the insubordination and insolence of many of the students. Andrew Massie, the senior regent at the Revolution of 1688–9, dictated his notes rapidly without stopping to explain points of difficulty, so that few of his students paid any attention to him. Those who did not stay away from his class, spent their time 'talking, tossing, and fighting together', so that regents in adjoining rooms could not get on with their work. For more than a generation after the Restoration, the College authorities were more preoccupied with the maintenance of discipline than with the academic attainments of their students. Angry young men, whether Presbyterian or Episcopalian, seized upon ancient customs such as throwing in the ball to the bajan (first year) classroom or boxing at the College gate in order to turn into political demonstrations what had originally been student high-jinks tolerated by the authorities.

The high-water mark here was the ceremony on Christmas Day 1680 when the students, led by an Englishman, Robert Brown, who described himself as 'Secretary of State to all our Theatrical and Extra-literal Divertisements', succeeded in publicly burning an effigy of the Pope, in spite of the combined resistance of the College authorities, the town guard, and the regular troops. As this was at the

A MODEST
APOLOGY
FOR THE
Students of Edenburgh
BURNING A
POPE
DECEMBER 25. 1680.

Humbly Refcuing the Actors from the Imputation of
Difloyalty and Rebellion, with which they were charged in a
LETTER, &c.

——Manet alt² mente repoftum
Convitium Papæ, fpretiq; injuria.——

LONDON:

Printed for *Richard Janeway*, in *Queens-Head Alley* in
Pater-Nofter-Row : 1681.

14. Title-page of a pamphlet defending the students who had burned an
effigy of the Pope at the time of the Popish Plot.

15. Two further drawings from Flint's notes showing students playing games.

height of the excitement over the Popish plot, and as the Duke of York, heir presumptive to the crown and a notorious Papist, was in residence at Holyrood at the time, the Privy Council charged the students concerned with treason and closed the College. Its re-opening was conditional on bonds being given by the youths and their parents for the students' good behaviour. For some years after the Revolution each regent was instructed to obtain the signatures of all his students to a solemn declaration that they would behave themselves, not try to continue barbarous customs which promoted disorder such as throwing in the ball to the bajans, and agree in advance to the sentence of expulsion being pronounced against them if they failed to honour their promises.

How students spent their scanty leisure is not very clear from the available evidence. The College rules consist chiefly of prohibitions. Students must not stand at the College gate nor trouble other students by shouldering or tossing. They must not throw stones or snowballs or play in the courts or yards when classes were in session. The speaking of Scots or English was strictly forbidden, though early in eighteenth century we hear that 'the speaking of English and not Latin is become customary, and cursing and swearing is too ordinary without any due punishment'. By this time too 'the office of hebdomadar is much neglected', and it was difficult to get the student censors to delate their classmates for breaches of the rules.

Ball games were certainly played in the afternoons or evenings on the College playing fields. Possibly inspired by St Andrews practice, the town council in 1673 set up a pair of butts 'for the colleginers recreation' at the back of the Teviot chambers and provided a silver arrow for competition. There were also facilities in the town to learn shorthand, fencing, dancing, and riding and to study subjects not taught at the University such as French, Dutch, German, and (sometimes) Polish. The projectors of the Nonconformist College to be established at Edinburgh insisted that such facilities were essential if English students were to be attracted to Edinburgh. Catchpuls, where tennis was played, existed and resort to them was not forbidden by the rules of 1701, although it had been earlier. Billiard rooms were also discouraged by the authorities but continued to be frequented, and it was a source of complaint in 1704 that the College fabric was 'greatly damnified by students playing at racketts and hand balls'.

It was now becoming possible for a student, by subscribing to the funds of the College Library, to read books there and even to 'carry a book out with him'. It was, however, an exceptional student who, like Sir Robert Sibbald, 'from the time I entered the College, any money I got, I did employ it for buying books'. Students and regents, on the specious plea that no provision for meals was made in the College, frequented the neighbouring taverns. Some of them drank to excess, especially when the College porter provided facilities on the premises and probably made his own liquor, while others visited the houses of ill-fame which tended to spring up in proximity to the College. Red gowns, recommended by the Commission of 1690 to prevent 'vageing and vice', were not worn at Edinburgh.

(2)

The Eighteenth
Century

NATIONAL POLITICS AND THE UNIVERSITY

THE ecclesiastico-political conflicts which dominated Scotland in the seventeenth century had extended to the universities. The upsurge of Presbyterianism in the 1630s was followed by the dismissal of two Episcopalian regents, while the Restoration of Episcopacy after 1660 cost some Presbyterian masters dear and prevented many students from taking degrees. The glorious Revolution of 1688 was followed by what was known in Episcopalian circles as the 'Presbyterian Inquisition', which transformed Edinburgh from an Episcopalian college, with one or two masters who had hobnobbed with the Jesuits, into a Presbyterian seminary. Whereas St Andrews continued its addiction to Jacobitism well into the eighteenth century, Edinburgh was pre-eminently the Whig University of Scotland. Exceptional measures were taken in the 1690s not only to eliminate Jacobitism and Episcopalianism, but to abolish outlets for student high spirits which could be exploited and transformed into political demonstrations by those who disliked the Whig and Presbyterian establishment. Similarly when loyal citizens, obeying the town council's behest, illuminated their windows to celebrate Queen Mary's birthday 'colleginers' and apprentices broke their windows and were arrested by the town guard.

Immediately after the Revolution the needs of the College, notably a confirmation and extension of its ancient privileges, and compensation for the loss of its share of the bishops' revenues upon the restoration of Episcopacy in 1661, were placed before the town council by the masters. In their opinion money was urgently required to settle new professions of law and physic, enrich the Library, augment the salaries of regents, build lodgings for regents and chambers for students, as well as to complete Burnet's steeple. The town council were sufficiently impressed to send the Lord Provost to London to present a congratulatory address to William III and Mary II and to represent the affairs of both town and College to the Sovereigns. Although William's reply that it was a Parliament only which could furnish a suitable relief was discouraging, he undertook to recommend the city's case to the next Parliament. In the end, no doubt largely owing to the influence of William III's friend and adviser, William Carstares, a substantial grant was made to the College, but it was not earmarked for the uses upon which the masters had proposed to spend it. Instead it was applied to found the Chair of Ecclesiastical History and to provide stipends for Divinity bursars. After Carstares became principal of the College in 1703, a further government grant was received from Queen Anne. These two grants were the first permanent and substantial gifts from the central government which Edinburgh had received since James VI's donation of the teinds of Currie in the first days of the College. Carstares through his influence at Court had seen to it that Presbyterianism and Whiggery had reaped their due reward.

The accession of the House of Hanover confirmed the existing tradition and was soon followed by an Act of Parliament which allowed the town council to collect local excise duties and apply the proceeds to paying the salaries of professors in the University, including the professor of Civil History and the holders of some Law Chairs. The practice grew up of presenting loyal addresses to the Crown on auspicious occasions and also of publicly announcing the devotion of the University to the Sovereign in times of danger and disturbance. The University of Edinburgh it is claimed was among the first public bodies to address her Majesty Queen Anne and to testify their zeal and loyalty to her person and government at the time of a Jacobite attempt to invade Scotland in 1708. But the first of these occasions to be recorded in the surviving College minutes occurred in May 1736, when a short and formal address was presented to George II by the Lord Provost, who was also MP for the city, congratulating him on the marriage of the Prince of Wales. Shortly after, Leonard Howard, Chaplain to the Prince of Wales, was given an honorary MA.

In October 1736, just six weeks after the lynching of Captain Porteous by an Edinburgh mob, the Senatus ordered coaches at the Laigh Coffee House to convey its members on a formal visit to the Earl of Ilay, the manager of government business in Scotland, thus demonstrating in the most public manner possible, the University's support for Walpole's administration. The declaration of war between Britain and France in 1744, and French plans to invade Britain and support the Jacobites, were the occasion of another loyal address to George II, which promised 'most strenuous opposition in our stations to all attempts in favour of Popery and arbitrary power' and promised 'to instil the same principles of duty and loyalty into the minds of the youth under our inspection'.

The arrival of Bonnie Prince Charlie in the city gave the professors and students an opportunity they probably had not anticipated of living up to their professions. No meeting of Senatus is recorded between 18 June 1745 and 12 December 1746, classes were suspended and some professors and many students were active on the Hanoverian side. Charles Mackie, professor of History and a stout Whig, went around spreading atrocity stories about the Jacobites and, when challenged, replied he did not give his own stories much credit, but thought 'telling them may have a good effect'. During the Seven Years' War, the professor of Greek was so fired with patriotism that his students had merely to bang on the wainscoting during a lecture for him to think he was hearing another salvo fired from the Castle to announce a glorious victory over the French. Anxious to hear details, he would hurriedly close his class and release his students ten or twelve minutes before the due time.

Under George III, the practice of addressing the Sovereign grew more frequent and the addresses were often routed through one of the Secretaries of State, preferably Dundas, who was also MP for

16. Principal William Carstares; detail from a painting by William Aikman, *c.* 1712.

Edinburghshire 1774–82 and 1783–90 and for the city from 1790 to 1802. When the French Revolution threw Britain into a ferment, Whiggery was transmuted into diehard Toryism. The loyal address, presented in 1792, referred to the excellent constitution established by the glorious Revolution and the Senate promised to labour 'with increased assiduity' to instil into their students 'just sentiments with respect to the nature of Society' [etc.]. One member of Senate, at least, meant what he said and David Hume, professor of Scots Law, occupied much of the Senate's time in 1799 with his complaint of the blasphemous and seditious discourses which were being delivered at meetings of the Speculative Society. One result of his notorious Toryism was that liberal-minded parents preferred to send their sons to Glasgow to study law under John Millar. Hume, in fact, went too far and failed to carry most of his colleagues with him. That his alarm was not entirely groundless had however been demonstrated by the riotous behaviour of a group of medical students in April 1794, when *The Royal Martyr* had been played at the Theatre Royal. Not only had they applauded republican sentiments: they had attempted to prevent the singing of the national anthem and, after a struggle, had been forcibly expelled from the theatre by the Tory spectators, with Sir Walter Scott well to the fore.

REFORM AND DEVELOPMENT

The unimpeachable Whiggery of the College in the first half of the eighteenth century provided an indispensable basis for its transformation. What had been in the seventeenth century a prosperous Arts College, with a small but respected Divinity school attached to it, became in the middle of the eighteenth century one of the leading universities of Europe. The process began with the abolition of the archaic regent system in 1708. Principal Carstares, with his experience of the new Dutch universities, was certainly responsible for this long overdue reform, which anticipated, in academic work, the principle of division of labour ascribed to Adam Smith. The university reformers of the sixteenth century had advocated but failed to establish it effectively. It had however been applied in practice to the Faculty of Divinity at Edinburgh before the end of the seventeenth century.

In Arts the process began with the establishment of a Chair of Mathematics, but this was not a compulsory subject. In 1708, instead of having four part-time professors of Greek, each of them also engaged in teaching all the branches of Philosophy, a full-time professor of Greek was appointed; and the town council ruled that the professor of Greek could no longer veto admission of students to the philosophy classes, 'though they have not been taught Greek by him'. At the same time the wide field of philosophical study was divided into three branches, each taught by a separate professor: (1) Logic and Metaphysics; (2) Ethics and Natural Philosophy; and (3) Pneumatics and Moral Philosophy. After studying Logic and Metaphysics for a year, students would tackle Ethics and Natural Philosophy in the second year of the Philosophy course. The third professor of Philosophy would not have charge of a class but would prelect on Pneumatics and Moral Philosophy and also give public lectures on Philosophy to all Arts students in the common hall.

Greek was now to be studied as a linguistic subject in its own right, not as a mere tool to philosophical studies, while Natural Philosophy moved away from Aristotle and began to develop into a Newtonian science. Even earlier than this while the 'poor wretches' at Cambridge according to William Whiston, 'were ignominiously studying the fictitious hypotheses of the Cartesian', the mathematical Gregories at Edinburgh were teaching and examining their students upon 'several branches of the Newtonian philosophy'.

The most important result of the abolition of the regent system was to enable students to choose the classes they meant to attend and take them in any order they pleased. By 1731 it was estimated that half of those in the first-year philosophy classes had not previously attended either the Latin or the Greek class. It was the quality and wide range of available courses and the absence of restriction upon student choice that attracted to Edinburgh a great concourse of students from home and abroad. And this in turn made possible further diversification of courses and faculties. In Arts new Chairs were established in Universal Civil History (1719) – that is, such history as was not taught by the senior professor of Ecclesiastical History – and in Rhetoric and Belles Lettres (1760).

The Faculty of Law with Chairs in Public Law, Civil Law, and Scots Law, and linked closely with the Arts Chair of Civil History, had been established by 1722; but a school which was based on Scots Law could not expect to attract many students furth of Scotland.

It was different with the Faculty of Medicine. The first Medical Chair had been established as early as 1685, but it seems very doubt-

17. A decorated capital letter from Flint's notes showing a regent lecturing in anatomy.

ful whether its holders, Sir Robert Sibbald, Dr James Halket, and Dr Archibald Pitcairne ever did any teaching in the College, although all of them were scholars as well as men of eminence in their profession. Similarly the titular professor of Botany, James Sutherland, occupied himself with the cultivation of the Physic Gardens and the instruction of pupils of the College of Surgeons in botany. By the end of the seventeenth century there were 'no less than five distinct physic gardens in Edinburgh'; but the real beginning of medical instruction in the College of Edinburgh was the appointment of Robert Eliot, who was already 'public dissector' to the College of Surgeons, as professor of Anatomy (1705). This was apparently the first appointment of its kind in Britain. Soon Dr Charles Alston was giving lectures not only in botany in general but specifically on *materia medica;* Dr James Crawford was elected as professor of Physick and Chemistry (1713), the very year in which a Chair of Chemistry was founded at Cambridge; and in 1720 Alexander Monro *primus* was appointed to the Anatomy Chair. In 1726 four Fellows of the College of Physicians were appointed professors of Medicine and Chemistry, sharing the various branches of these subjects between them by mutual agreement. All of them and some of their colleagues in allied subjects had studied at Leyden. About the same time a surgeon, who had specialised in Midwifery, was appointed to a Chair in this branch of Medicine.

By this time, then, the College was actually teaching anatomy and surgery, chemistry and medicine, institutes and practice of medicine, botany, and midwifery. From 1726 candidates for medical degrees were examined, not by the Fellows of the Colleges of Physicians or Surgeons, but by the University Faculty of Medicine. The practice of graduation by collective theses had already died out in Arts and candidates for the MD degree, after attending the prescribed classes, had to present an individual thesis and submit themselves to oral and practical examinations conducted by their professors.*

While no new Chairs were established in other existing faculties for nearly a century after 1760, several medical, surgical, and scientific Chairs were founded in the later eighteenth and early nineteenth centuries. Even then no attempt was made to establish a separate faculty of science and the older scientific Chairs continued to be linked either with the Arts Faculty, for example Natural Philosophy, or with the growing Medical School, for example Chemistry. In the later eighteenth century, when sharper lines of division were being drawn between Science and Medicine, new Chairs were founded, in rapid succession, in Natural History, Astronomy, and Agriculture. While Natural History was linked with Medicine, Astronomy and Agriculture were reckoned to belong to the Faculty of Arts.

By this time there were honorary doctorates in Divinity and Law, awarded by the Senatus to candidates approved by the respective faculties; but the only degrees awarded to students at the end of a regular course of instruction were in Arts and Medicine. In both faculties graduation was the exception – so much so in Arts that the Faculty was never very sure what the requirements were for an MA degree. When the curriculum to be imposed upon *gratis* students was considered in 1777, the Senate originally drew up a fixed order in which the seven subjects must be taken, but then accepted unanimously two amendments proposed by Professor Adam Ferguson, one demoting Rhetoric as 'a more recent institution' from a fixed place in the curriculum, and the other adding to the regulations the rider that

---

* For a fuller account of the development of a Medical Faculty see Douglas Guthrie, *The Medical School of Edinburgh* (Edinburgh, 1959).

'it may be necessary for students to accommodate the order of study to their several views and destinations'. It was then left to the Faculty to decide on his merits whether a particular candidate was qualified to enter on the course to which he solicited free admittance. As early as 1734 David Mallet *alias* Malloch, who had attended classes for three years, had worked diligently and had since published works which gave to the world 'sufficient proofs of his learning', was awarded the MA degree without any degree examination. Although in 1814 a regular order of study for those who wished to graduate was laid down, the Senatus continued to grant honorary MAs to former students who had not complied with the requirements for the ordinary degree. Sometimes in the early nineteenth century the degree was given as a prize to undergraduates who had distinguished themselves in essay-writing competitions.

In Medicine, on the other hand, the rules seem to have been more strictly enforced. In 1726, when the conduct of the examination was entrusted to the newly instituted Medical Faculty, each candidate was required to produce evidence that he had studied Medicine at Edinburgh or elsewhere for three years and had attended lectures in all the recognised departments of medical studies as well as clinical lectures at a hospital. Two months before graduation he must submit a thesis upon some branch of Medicine to one of the professors. The thesis was then revised by the candidate and submitted to the Faculty of Medicine: if it was approved, an oral examination by two professors, designed to test his proficiency in medical knowledge, followed. If the examiners were not satisfied, further tests took place in the presence of the Faculty. If these were satisfactory, the candidate printed his thesis and had, if challenged, to defend it publicly, although this was seldom, if ever, required in practice. The whole of these proceedings, oral and written, were conducted in Latin. These regulations, amended slightly in 1767, remained essentially unaltered until well into the nineteenth century.

At first there were often only one or two medical doctorates given in a year. By mid-century there were often a dozen or more; by the end of the century fifty was not uncommon and the number in the early nineteenth century regularly exceeded a hundred and once rose to 140. These figures, it should be noted, conceal the actual significance of the University of Edinburgh in the medical education of the

18. Title-page of MD thesis by Benjamin Rush.

DISSERTATIO PHYSICA
INAUGURALIS,
DE
COCTIONE CIBORUM
IN VENTRICULO:

QUAM,

ANNUENTE SUMMO NUMINE,

Ex Auctoritate Reverendi admodum Viri,

GULIELMI ROBERTSON, S. S. T. P.

ACADEMIÆ EDINBURGENÆ PRÆFECTI;

NEC NON

Ampliſſimi SENATUS ACADEMICI conſenſu,
Et nobiliſſimae FACULTATIS MEDICÆ decreto;

Pro GRADU DOCTORIS,

SUMMISQUE IN MEDICINA HONORIBUS ET PRIVILEGIIS
RITE ET LEGITIME CONSEQUENDIS;

Eruditorum examini ſubjicit

BENJAMINUS RUSH, A. M.

PENSYLVANIENSIS.

Prid. Id. Junii, hora locoque ſolitis.

Omnino, ſcientia ex naturae lumine petenda, non ex antiqui-
tatis obſcuritate. Nec refert, quid factum fuerit; illud
videndum, quid fieri poſſit. Verulam. Oper.

EDINBURGI:
Apud BALFOUR, AULD, et SMELLIE,
Academiae Typographos.

M,DCC,LXVIII.

eighteenth and nineteenth centuries. In this faculty, as in Arts, it was only a small minority of students who proceeded to graduation. While the average number of medical students in the seven years down to 1783 was 400 and in 1783–4 was over 500, only twenty-two students on an average took the M D degree, the only one available in Medicine. The great majority of the medical graduates in this period were Englishmen, Irishmen, or colonials, who had previously studied at other universities before coming to Edinburgh for a final year. Even between Arts and Medicine there was not yet a hard and fast dividing line. Many Edinburgh medical students attended Arts classes before starting on their medical course and not all the 400 or 500 young men who annually attended the Anatomy class intended to take up Medicine as a life work.

In the minutes of the Senatus Academicus, the first list of professors divided into faculties dates from 1785. The order was then Theology, Law, Medicine, and Arts. Within faculties the professors ranked according to seniority except in Divinity where, apart from the principal, who was also sometimes reckoned to be titular professor of Divinity, the order was first the Professor of Divinity, next the Regius professor of Ecclesiastical History, who is always described in the royal commission of appointment as 'second professor of divinity and third master in the College', and finally the professor of Oriental Languages. As second master of the College, the professor of Divinity presided over the Senate in the absence of the principal well into the nineteenth century. When the foundation stone of the present Old College was laid in 1789, the principal with the professor of Divinity on his right and the professor of Ecclesiastical History on his left, headed the academical body, although many of the other professors were of senior standing.

The pre-eminence of Divinity was also manifest in other ways. The Senatus in 1734 instructed the professor of Moral Philosophy to prelect every Monday morning 'upon the truth of the Christian religion' and if any books used in his class 'shall contain anything contrary to the scriptures or the Confession of Faith or to good manners, he shall confute the same to prevent the youths' being corrupted with error or immorality'. As late as 1735 the Senatus felt competent to try a Divinity student for heretical opinions and sentenced him to be publicly extruded from the University. If he repented and proved the sincerity of his repentance, he might later be allowed to return to the University and study in any faculty but Divinity. A few years later, the Senatus unanimously made representations to the town council against the establishment of a playhouse in Edinburgh.

Down to the middle of the eighteenth century the principal was still expected to give out a Latin theme each year for the bajans and a Greek one for the semi-class. Supported by his colleagues on the Senate, he also had a public prelection, attended by all students in the common hall, at the beginning of January when the venerable laws of the College were read and explained. The 1733 recension of these rules showed that changes were taking place. Classes were now to begin, not at seven (as in the 1701 version), but at eight o'clock each morning. Students were no longer required to speak to each other in Latin and the threat of corporal punishment for misconduct had been removed, while student censors were not now expected to delate their fellow students to the professors for misconduct.

Although Principal Robertson occasionally 'visited' the classes, by this time each professor was free to teach his subject as he thought fit. Latin was still used by a diminishing number as the language of their formal lectures and in the book kept in connection with Professor Stevenson's class of Logic, in which prize essays were entered from 1737 to 1751, about half were written in Latin, and the other half in English. Curiously enough Latin survived longest in the Faculty of Medicine. Graduation theses were composed solely in that language until 1833, when the Senatus permitted the use either of Latin or English. In 1834 a few theses were presented in Latin, but from 1835 onwards all theses were written in English, except for an occasional one presented by a foreign student who preferred to make use of Latin. About the same time, the final examination for the MD degree ceased to be in Latin; and, as a substitute, 'a previous examination', designed to test all candidates' competent knowledge of the Latin language, was introduced.

THE PROFESSORS

Perhaps the most satisfying explanation of the eminence of the University of Edinburgh in the second half of the eighteenth century lies in the ability and devotion of its teachers and the width and flexibility of its curriculum. It could never challenge Oxford in Classics or Cambridge in Mathematics. If a few holders of classical Chairs at Edinburgh in this period are remembered at all, it is not for their professional expertise. Andrew Dalzel continued, while professing

Greek, the history of the University begun by the seventeenth-century 'humanity regent', Thomas Craufurd. It was Dalzel who secured from the Lord Lyon the grant of a coat of arms for the University in 1789 and had a seal bearing these arms engraved for use on diplomas, which had hitherto been issued with 'one of the city seals', usually a seal of cause, attached. In 1787, too, Dalzel, as librarian, had to report to the Senate the theft of the College mace. Convinced that Deacon Brodie, one of their own number, was responsible for the theft, the town council, two years later, presented to the College a new and beautifully designed silver mace, which is still carried by the *bedellus* on ceremonial occasions.

The outstanding Edinburgh mathematician of the century, Colin McLaurin, died young, reputedly from overwork on the fortification of Edinburgh to resist Bonnie Prince Charlie in 1745. His successor died a bankrupt after embezzling University funds entrusted to his care; and neither Dugald Stewart nor Adam Ferguson has a place in the history of mathematics. It is a different story when we come to the newer disciplines. Newtonian physics were taught at Edinburgh earlier than at Cambridge and John Robison's thirty years' tenure of the Chair of Natural Philosophy gave it additional lustre. Charles Mackie, the first professor of Universal Civil History was the master both of Hume and Robertson, though none of those who followed him in the eighteenth century was a worthy successor. Similarly, Hugh Blair, the first professor of Rhetoric, during his twenty-two years in the Chair, enjoyed a great reputation as a teacher.

On the Arts side, however, the outstanding teachers were professors of Philosophy. Sir John Pringle soon gave up his Philosophy Chair to study the diseases of the army and to become President of the Royal Society. The earliest to make his mark as a teacher was John Stevenson, who discarded Aristotle for Locke and made use of the historical method in teaching Philosophy. It was, however, his lectures on Rhetoric and Literary Criticism which made the deepest impression on his students and contributed most to the intellectual renaissance of eighteenth-century Edinburgh. We have the authority of Bower for saying that no other Edinburgh professor 'had the honour of training up so many young men to a love of letters, and who afterwards made so distinguished a figure in the literary world'. In the course of 'visiting' the classes during his first year as principal, Robertson, who

19. Professor Adam Ferguson; detail from a painting by William Millar, 1763.

20. Professor Dugald Stewart; a drawing by John Henning, 1811.

had been the favourite pupil of Stevenson, paid a graceful and well-deserved tribute to his old professor. Stevenson had, at the end of his career, as a junior colleague in the Moral Philosophy Chair, Adam Ferguson, who was renowned equally as professor, author, and man of affairs. Nowadays he is best remembered as one of the founders of sociology. Ferguson was succeeded in the Moral Philosophy Chair by a pupil of his own, Dugald Stewart, who held the Chair for a quarter of a century, during which time he was the most influential advocate and exponent of the common sense school of philosophy. Like Ferguson, he was attracted by border-line subjects, including Aesthetics, Psychology, and Political Economy. The roll of his pupils included

21. Professor Alexander Monro *primus*; engraved in 1775 by James Basire from the painting by Allan Ramsay.

two destined to become prime ministers, Palmerston and Russell, and the founders of the *Edinburgh Review*; divines such as Dr Thomas Chalmers, the leader of the 'Disruption'; historians such as Sir Archibald Alison and James Mill; judges such as Lord Cockburn, who wrote 'to me his lectures were like the opening of the heavens! I felt that I had a soul'; and Sir Walter Scott himself, the wizard of the North.

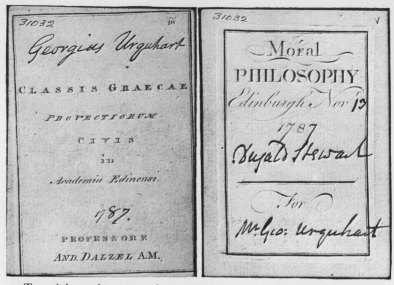

22. Two eighteenth-century class cards.

Neither the Divinity nor the Law professors, except perhaps for the professor of Scots Law from 1786 to 1822, David Hume, were men of mark; but the record of the Arts Faculty was equalled, if not excelled, by that of the Faculty of Medicine in this period. Best known are the three generations of professors of Anatomy, all named Alexander Monro, who held this Chair in unbroken succession from 1720 to 1846. The first Monro had begun teaching with a handful of students; when he died in 1767 the number had risen to over 400 and continued to rise until well into the nineteenth century. While it is customary to treat him as the Father of the Edinburgh Medical School, Dr Douglas Guthrie considers that his father John Monro 'in whose fertile brain the idea originated' has a better claim to this title. The first Monro was a great teacher and founded in 1731 the 'Society for the Improvement of Medical Knowledge', one of the precursors of the Royal Society of Edinburgh, but did little else to advance the study of his subject. His son, the second Monro had 'all the advantages of a great orator'* and made fundamental contributions to modern anatomy, especially his discovery, disputed by William Hunter of Glasgow, of

---

* Topham, *Letters from Edinburgh*, p. 215.

23. Professor Joseph Black lecturing to his students; from Kay's
Old Edinburgh Portraits, 1787.

the functions of the lymphatic vessels, and his exposition of the structure of the nervous system. Like his colleague Black, although he
demonstrated his discoveries in lecturing to his students, he was slow
to publish them and thus became involved in controversies over
priority of discovery. He began at Edinburgh the study of comparative anatomy.

Two great scientists, William Cullen and Joseph Black, filled the
Chemistry Chair from 1755 to 1795. Cullen was primarily interested
in Chemistry in relation to Medicine, giving pioneer clinical lectures
in the Royal Infirmary and transferring to the Chair of Institutes of

Medicine (or Physiology) in 1766. According to Bower, 'the bold enterprising genius of Cullen . . . shook the pillars that supported the system of Boerhaave. His *First Lines of the Practice of Physic* produced a powerful sensation not in this country only, but throughout Europe'. A lay auditor found his lectures clear but insipid, although admitting that they showed also 'his profound knowledge of the mysteries of his profession'; but to a would-be physician they were as entertaining as they were instructive. Cullen's published works were essentially text-books for medical students, long since disused, and polemical works against a rival teacher, John Brown, who had devised the Brunonian theory of medicine. His successor Black, on the other hand, was a brilliant research chemist. His thesis for the degree of M D at Edinburgh exploded the phlogiston theory of oxidation and proved, by quantitative experiment, that limestone when heated did not gain anything from the fire, but lost weight owing to the expulsion of 'fixed air', that is, carbon dioxide. Before he was appointed to the Edinburgh Chemistry Chair, Black had discovered the principle of latent heat, and he continued his researches while he was professor of Chemistry, although his results were not published until after his death. Although Black was no orator and his delivery was sometimes halting, 'no chemist was ever more successful in his experiments'.* Both Black and Cullen kept in touch with the developing industrial centres in the north of England and made valuable contributions to industrial technology.

John Hope, who occupied the Chair of Botany from 1761 to 1786, encouraged his students to explore the Highlands and bring back botanical discoveries, gave help and advice to Pennant in arranging his famous *Tour,* and deputed one of his promising students to conduct Lightfoot, the author of the first *Flora* of Scotland, to places where he would find rare plants. His interests were not confined to botany, but covered the whole realm of natural history. It was he who persuaded the commissioners on the forfeited estates to spend money on sending a young gardener from the Edinburgh Physic Garden on a series of scientific tours of Scotland, from which he returned laden with botanical, geological, and other specimens for the College museum. This museum, which had long been one of the show places in the College, ceased to be a chance assemblage of curiosities and rarities and was transformed into a scientific collection of objects which were

---

* Ibid., p. 214.

24. Professor John Hope visiting the Physic Garden; from Kay's *Old Edinburgh Portraits*, 1786.

used to illustrate Hope's lectures to his students. In 1767 the govern-ment instituted a Regius Chair of Natural History, and John Walker, the second Regius professor, although something of a pluralist, fol-lowed in Hope's footsteps. Daniel Rutherford, who succeeded Hope in the Botany Chair, is remembered mainly for his discovery of the gas nitrogen.

If the pre-clinical teaching was of a high quality, the peculiar glory of the eighteenth-century Medical School was its clinical teaching, although it should be remembered that this was at first limited to Medicine and did not extend to Surgery. The Edinburgh physicians and surgeons combined to raise funds by a public appeal and the Royal Infirmary of Edinburgh, sited in a 'small hired house' at the head of Robertson's Close in the Cowgate, with beds for only six patients, opened its doors in 1729. In 1736 the 'Surgeons' Hospital' in College Wynd was established. The grant of a royal charter in 1736 to the Infirmary was speedily followed by the erection of a new building, designed to receive 240 patients, and including a surgical theatre in which 200 students could be accommodated. Opened in 1741, the new Infirmary soon served as an emergency hospital where soldiers wounded in the Jacobite rising of 1745, or falling sick during the campaign, were attended to. John Rutherford, professor of Medicine from 1724 to 1747, described admirably the method followed by himself and his successors in giving courses of lectures on clinical medicine:

> I shall examine every Patient capable of appearing before you, that no circumstance may escape you, and proceed in the following manner: 1st, Give you a history of the disease. 2ndly, Enquire into the Cause. 3rdly, Give you my Opinion how it will terminate. 4thly, lay down the indications of cure yt arise, and if any new Symptoms happen acquaint you them, that you may see how I vary my prescriptions. And 5thly, Point out the different Method of Cure. If at any time you find me de-ceived in giving my Judgement, you'll be so good as to excuse me, for neither do I pretend to be, nor is the Art of Physic infallible, what you can in Justice expect from me is, some ac-curate observations and Remarks upon Diseases.*

---

* MS. Notes of Rutherford's Clinical Lectures in the Royal College of Physicians' Library, Edinburgh, p. 7, quoted from Comrie, *History of Scottish Medicine*, I, p. 306.

The Governors of the Infirmary agreed in 1769 to provide similar lectures on surgical cases. Rutherford's successor, Robert Whytt, taught both the theory and practice of medicine for twenty years, carried out research into the cure of the stone and of nervous disorders, published important physiological treatises, and gave the first clear clinical account of tuberculous meningitis. John Gregory, a member of the most famous professorial family in Scottish history, and William Cullen became joint professors of Medicine, it being understood that each should teach the theory and the practice in alternate years. Gregory's death in 1773 brought this experiment to an end and his son, James Gregory, was elected professor of the institutes of medicine or physiology in 1776. James Gregory published a Latin text-book on physiology at the beginning of his professorial career, proved a good teacher and was transferred in 1790, on the death of Cullen, to the Chair of Medicine, which he held with distinction until his death in 1821. A foreign visitor in 1810–11 described him as lecturing 'seated in the centre of a vast amphitheatre, covered with 500 heads, his hat on, and playing with the case of his spectacles'. He spoke without notes and 'in a tone of conversation', while his students 'manifested their interest, from time to time, by a little murmur of applause, which the professor checked by a motion of his hand, and went on'.* Outside of the Medical Faculty he is remembered, if at all, as the original prescriber of 'Gregory's powder'.

An important addition to the original Medical Faculty was the Chair of Midwifery, which, founded by the town council in 1726, became a College Chair in 1739. The first two professors taught both midwives and medical students and the third professor of Midwifery, Thomas Young, emphasised both the clinical and the systematic aspects of his subject and founded the Edinburgh School of Obstetrics. By this time there was a lying-in ward at the Royal Infirmary; and Young's successor, Alexander Hamilton, was able to establish a separate lying-in hospital in 1791.

The institution of clinical lectures in surgery at the Royal Infirmary led to attempts to establish a College Chair of Surgery; but this was defeated by Monro *secundus*, who insisted that this subject was included in his commission. A separate Chair in Materia Medica was, however, established in 1768 and the first incumbent, Francis Home, made important contributions to science as well as to medicine. His

---

* L. Simond, *Journal of a Tour and Residence in Great Britain*, I, pp. 377–8.

experiments on bleaching won the approval of the Board of Trustees for Fisheries and Manufactures, while his applications of chemistry to agriculture, based on his research to prove that plants abstracted nourishment from the air, won for him a gold medal from the Edinburgh Society for the Improvement of Arts and Manufactures. When serving as an army surgeon in the Low Countries, he had insisted that water should be boiled before it was drunk by the troops for whose health he was responsible, and as a professor he made the first scientific study of *croup,* the deadly disease which came to be known as diphtheria. In Medicine, as in Arts, the great names of the eighteenth century were, in the main, themselves Edinburgh students.

Quite apart from the success of the town council in choosing on the whole the best candidates for appointment to vacant Chairs, there was another reason for the vigour and assiduity of Edinburgh professors in discharging their duties in a century when men were all too ready to transform offices into sinecures. This is to be found in the financial arrangements which Edinburgh shared with the other Scottish universities. Professors at the English universities received fixed salaries and, broadly speaking, the fewer students they attracted the better they were pleased. At the Scottish universities, while tenure was as secure as in England, basic salaries were tiny and the professors had to exert themselves to secure a living wage. Many of them made money by their pens. Arnot, in his eighteenth-century *History of Edinburgh,* attributed to increased literary earnings the fact that Edinburgh professors in the years around 1783 could afford to keep their carriages, which none could afford to do twenty years earlier.

But much more important was the arrangement by which each professor collected, in advance, and retained for his own use, a fee from every student who wished to attend his lectures. This system was probably coeval with the origin of the University and there are suggestions in the seventeenth century that professors were expected to content themselves with a fixed salary, while the regents supplemented their incomes by collecting fees from students. These sums varied according to the parents' means. Men of wealth like Sir John Foulis of Ravelston gave his son's regent, during his four years' course from 1689 to 1693, between £20 and £30 (Scots) each year. On the other hand, more than once in the seventeenth century, the town council decided that the regents must instruct poor students without trying to exact fees from them. The end of the regent system and other changes in the structure of the University soon obliterated the

25. An Anatomy class card. Between the feet of the figure can be seen the octagonal New Anatomy Theatre built in 1764.

distinction between professors and regents. For at least a century and
a half nearly all Edinburgh professors relied for the major part of
their incomes on the fees paid over to them by their students. At least
in the eighteenth century prices were relatively stable, taxation was
minimal and wages were low.

Every additional student enrolled represented a clear profit of
three guineas, which was the recognised fee for a first attendance at
classes both in Arts and Medicine. Poor students, at least in Arts,
continued to receive *gratis* tickets and it was often suggested that
professors were too lax in issuing these. All others paid a standard fee
of two guineas, or, in some cases, three guineas, for each class they
attended. The chief beneficiaries from this system were the favoured
Medical professors, especially of Chemistry and Anatomy, whose
courses were regularly attended by hundreds of students each year.
Able and energetic professors in Arts also had no difficulty in attracting large and profitable classes in the second half of the eighteenth
century. The disappearance of graduation as a normal feature of the
Arts course allowed students to bypass unpopular professors and
attend more than once courses of lectures by the favoured few.

In the Faculty of Law, few, if any, professors could hope to attract
a large audience and consequently there were times when some of the
Law professors ceased to lecture and turned their chairs into sinecures. The teaching of law was so closely linked with Scottish practice
that it was unattractive to students who did not mean to pursue their
professional careers in Scotland. In Divinity, class fees were not
exacted. This may be explained either as a survival in a conservative
faculty of the seventeenth-century distinction between regents and
professors or as a recognition that it was beyond the resources of most
Divinity students to pay such annual fees to their professors. The
result was that the Divinity professors had to supplement their meagre
salaries and lack of fees by finding other employment. Most of them
served as parish ministers or at least preached regularly in the
Edinburgh churches.

The inadequacy of professorial salaries in Law and Divinity was
not the only drawback to a system based on payment by results. It
naturally led to bad feeling between the less popular professors, struggling to get together a reasonably sized class, and their more successful competitors. This was probably the underlying cause of many of
the disputes over changes in class hours and it certainly produced
opposition by vested interests to new departures which would have

been beneficial to the University. Moreover, professors who wished to institute advanced classes were sometimes thwarted by colleagues who feared that such courses would compete for a limited student demand with their own already established classes.

These and other drawbacks became more apparent in the nineteenth century. In the eighteenth the system was warmly approved by practical administrators like Principal Robertson, who was in a good position to judge, and even in the nineteenth it was held up as an example to England by would-be university reformers such as Coleridge, who preferred to make professors work to earn a decent salary, rather than to encourage them to treat their chairs as sinecures. Boerhaave, the famous Dutch professor of Medicine, when the Edinburgh Medical School was beginning to rival his own, wished God would send the Edinburgh professors larger salaries since this would make them less active and dangerous competitors.

An eighteenth-century Chair in any faculty was a part-time appointment. Here again the divines and the lawyers were at a disadvantage, unless they followed the principal's example and published historical best-sellers. The Arts professors could earn large sums by writing the right kind of books, preferably histories, for which there was an insatiable demand in the later eighteenth century. The Medical professors, though less likely to make large profits from their text-books, were all free to engage in private practice and regularly put the claims of their patients before the needs of their students.

Many professors, and especially those with established reputations, further supplemented their incomes by accepting as boarders in their own houses the sons of parents who could afford to pay handsomely for the privilege. It was believed that this solved at one stroke the recurring English objections to the leading Scottish universities – the absence of scholastic and moral supervision once the student had left the classroom, and the danger to delicately nurtured students' health from unscrupulous landladies, who were likely to fail to air beds and to provide adequate meals. Early in the eighteenth century Professor William Hamilton made a regular practice of taking boarders and explained on one occasion in 1725 to Baron Clerk that Clerk's son would have to share a room with one of Hamilton's sons or with another boarder, Lord Leven's son. If Clerk's son had had a governor then the practice would have been for pupil and governor to share a room. Later in the century Dugald Stewart's house seems to have contained a remarkable assortment of young English aristocrats.

26. David Hume; detail from the painting by Allan Ramsay, 1766.

THE STUDENTS

Turning from the great teachers to the men they taught, the difficulty in drawing up a list of Edinburgh students who won fame is to know where to draw the line. James Bruce and Mungo Park head the roll of African explorers. James Hutton may be regarded as 'the founder of the modern style of geology'. The zoologists and botanists include Erasmus Darwin, grandfather of the more famous author of the *Origin of Species*. Robert Adam, John Rennie, who regarded his time at the College as 'the three most profitable years of his life', and Robert Stevenson, the pioneer builder of lighthouses, head the list of architects and engineers. The lawyers are led by two Lord Chancellors, Wedderburn and Brougham, but better remembered in Scotland is Duncan Forbes of Culloden. Two prime ministers, Palmerston and Russell, head the roll of politicians, and Henry Dundas, in the previous generation, was Pitt's right-hand man in the Revolutionary and

Napoleonic Wars. Sir Ralph Abercromby, victor at Aboukir, and Thomas Cochrane, Earl of Dundonald, are perhaps the most notable members of the fighting services.

But the blossoming of the eighteenth-century University is most marked in the various branches of literature. Here the giants are David Hume, Walter Scott, and that prince of biographers, James Boswell. The poets include Robert Blair and James Thomson, John Leyden and Thomas Campbell. While John Home's drama *Douglas* was a short-lived *succès de scandale,* Oliver Goldsmith's plays are still performed on the commercial stage. Sir James Steuart pioneered the systematic study of political economy; Henry Mackenzie wrote *The Man of Feeling;* and James Mill, father of John Stuart Mill, is still remembered in his own right as philosopher and historian. The Reverend Alexander 'Jupiter' Carlyle and Lord Cockburn are the outstanding representatives of a class of authors whose autobiographical works merge into history. Sir John Sinclair, a voluminous controversialist in his own day, also edited that invaluable reference work, the *First Statistical Account of Scotland.* More akin to popular journalism are the essays of Lord Kames. Sir James Mackintosh's opinions on the French Revolution are still remembered. Francis Jeffrey and Francis Horner were closely associated with the early days of the *Edinburgh Review.* One of the great pioneers of adult education, George Birkbeck, has given his name to one of the constituent Colleges of the University of London. The Edinburgh students, notably the divines, lawyers, and physicians, who became professors in the University are not mentioned here. Thomas Boston wrote the *Crook in the Lot* and the *Fourfold State,* probably the religious works which were most widely read in eighteenth-century Scotland. The notorious writer on Deism, John Toland, and John Willis, who assisted his father to treat the mad King George III during the Regency crisis of 1788-9, were both Edinburgh graduates.*

Quantitatively the best evidence of the role played by the eighteenth-century University of Edinburgh is to be found in the first chapter of Dr Nicholas Hans's work, *New Trends in Education in the 18th century* (London, 1951). Dr Hans starts with the 5,500 persons, born between 1685 and 1785, who are included in the *Dictionary of National Biography.* Discarding a few criminals and freaks and nearly 2,000 men who did

---

* These paragraphs are based on *Viri Illustres,* ed. Patrick Geddes (Edinburgh, 1884).

not attend any school, and became famous through practical application of their natural talents, as sailors, soldiers, surgeons, architects, musicians, painters, or craftsmen, Dr Hans is left with 3,500 men of national repute. Most of them are clergymen, teachers, physicians, or lawyers; some are statesmen, inventors, reformers, and authors. More than 2,500 out of these 3,500 studied at a university as shown below:.

Oxford	842
Cambridge	777
Edinburgh	343
Trinity College Dublin	170
Glasgow	144
Aberdeen	109
St Andrews	54
Leyden	52
Other foreign universities	68

It will be noted that Edinburgh, judged by quantitative standards, can claim more distinguished alumni in this period than the other Scottish universities put together (343 against 307) and is not disgraced when her performance is compared with that of the ancient English universities. The reasons are not far to seek. Dr Hans points out that only three men, produced by Scottish schools and included in his statistics, completed their education in England, whereas not less than 152 out of 343 students at Edinburgh were English (and not less than 74 out of 307 at the other Scottish universities).

So far as Edinburgh University is concerned a still more remarkable result is shown by Dr Hans's analysis of the educational careers of 680 'scientists' of the seventeenth and eighteenth centuries, of whom 539 were Fellows of the Royal Society. This includes doctors and surgeons, archaeologists, historians, and economists as well as pure and applied scientists. Of these, in the seventeenth century, Oxford produced 56, Cambridge 41, Edinburgh 6, and the other Scottish universities 8; but in the following century the numbers were 60, 85, 79, and 32 respectively. Here Edinburgh had for a time outdistanced Oxford and was running neck and neck with Cambridge. In the opinion of Thomas Jefferson in 1789 so far as science was concerned 'no place in the World can pretend to a competition with Edinburgh'.*

---

* Jefferson to Dugald Stewart in *Papers of Thomas Jefferson*, xv, p. 204. I am indebted to my colleague Dr James V. Compton for this reference.

It may well be that these figures provide the basic explanation for the outstanding place of Edinburgh University in the intellectual life of the eighteenth century. While nearly half of her alumni thought worthy of inclusion in the DNB came from English homes, practically no Scottish born and educated students went to English universities— and the few who did, if they were interested in things of the mind, usually wished they had not.

This massive influx of English students and English influences into the Scottish universities, and pre-eminently into Edinburgh, was not new. As we have seen, the Tounis College had no sooner opened its doors in 1583 than English students began to study and graduate at what was then to them a foreign university. As late as the beginning of the eighteenth century the bulk of the English students at Edinburgh were nonconformists, who could not conscientiously have taken the religious tests imposed upon their students and graduates by the English universities.

No religious or political tests were imposed upon those who came to study at Edinburgh from countries furth of Scotland. Anglican and Presbyterian, Baptist and Quaker, Unitarian and Deist were equally welcome to all faculties except Divinity; and even the Faculty of Divinity, under the influence of Robertson's 'moderatism' gave the degree of Doctor of Divinity in 1779 to Robert Bell, who is described in the official record as 'minister of the Episcopal chapel in Edinburgh'. Whatever their religious beliefs, these English and Irish students came almost invariably from solid middle-class homes. Even in the later eighteenth century, Edinburgh had little to offer to an English aristocrat, although she did attract at this time a larger proportion of the scions of Scottish noble families than at any other period in her history. Palmerston and Russell were by no means the only English aristocrats to study at Edinburgh, but the percentage of aristocrats in the body of English and Irish students was infinitesimal. Sir John Carr attributed this to 'the extraordinary facility with which in Scotland the matrimonial yoke may, by a little stratagem, be imposed upon a young man';* but, much more important, was the fact that Oxford and Cambridge still provided what English aristocrats desired as an alternative to or as a preparation for the Grand Tour.

The shortest and most satisfying answer to what these sons of English squires, prosperous merchants, and well-to-do clergymen

---

* *Caledonian Sketches,* p. 94.

expected to gain from attending the University of Edinburgh is supplied by a contemporary journalist, Edward Topham, in his *Letters
from Edinburgh written in the years 1774 and 1775* (London, 1776). The
professors set their students 'an example of civility and good manners
as of morality and virtue . . . though all of them are men of letters,
and skilled in the sciences they profess, they are not less acquainted
with the world, and with polite behaviour, than with polite literature'
(p. 205). The number of these professors has been 'so augmented that
nothing is wanting to form a complete academical education' (p. 207),
and 'every age and rank [of student] have a liberty of choosing such
lectures as are most suited to their inclinations, pleasures, or pursuits
in life' (p. 210).

An Edinburgh education was not regarded as a training for the
higher flights of scholarship, but as a useful preparation for the practical
affairs of life. Lady Mary Wortley Montagu's views on the uselessness
or worse of the English universities from this point of view was shared
by many English and Irish parents. At Edinburgh on the contrary
'no particular study or science is in higher estimation than another:
all are taught; each has its votaries; and a proper portion of time is
allotted to those inferior qualifications, which we every day see assist
the greater accomplishments in the acquisition of reputation and
fortune. [Lacking deep knowledge of any one subject, the Scots excel]
the English as courtiers and men of the world; because they are always well stored with such acquisitions as render them more service-
able in society; and from which the most common occasions of life
may reap some advantage'.*

It is also possible, though I have not come across any contemporary
evidence of this, that relative cheapness was a subsidiary factor in
choice, in spite of what Topham and others call the extravagance of
English and especially Irish students at Edinburgh. There were the
inevitable chronic complaints about the extortions of the Edinburgh
landladies, voiced by the American medical student Benjamin Rush
in 1768 and by many others. At least one medical student from
America set out to recover his expenses by marrying an English heiress
and succeeded in acquiring as his wife a niece of a governor of the
Bank of England. Then, far more than now, the cost of a university
education was what the student–and his parental backer–cared to
make it. Many Scottish bursars thought themselves well off on £10 a

---

* Topham, *Letters from Edinburgh,* pp. 219–20.

year, though they presumably supplemented their bursaries by coach-
ing their fellow students and in other ways. Indeed, the greater
opportunities which Edinburgh afforded for part-time employment
was one reason why the University attracted an increasing proportion
of able but impecunious students who might otherwise have been
content to attend one of the other Scottish universities nearer to their
homes. Principal Lee told the Royal Commission of 1826 how one
student had spent on an average over two sessions only 6s. 9d. a week,
or £8 2s. during a session of twenty-four weeks, although he did
receive some food from the country occasionally. While an economical
student from Yorkshire in 1771 believed he could exist at Edinburgh
on £16 for half a year, a Virginian aristocrat estimated his reasonable
expenses at £120 *per annum*.

While relative cheapness may well have entered into parental
calculations, a more important factor was that English and Scottish
parents were no longer so impressed by the virtues of an education in
the Low Countries. This is confirmed by the figures collected by Dr
Hans, which show that only 120 out of over 2,500 DNB notabilities
born between 1685 and 1785 had any part of their education at
foreign universities. Edinburgh in the eighteenth century had taken
the place Leyden occupied in the seventeenth. It offered much the
same lecture courses, treated in much the same manner; it was, in
spite of contemporary diatribes about British roads, easier of access;
and as Latin ceased to be the language of instruction in continental
universities a new language barrier arose which restricted the choice
of many English students and forced them, if they wished to have a
modern university education at all, to come to the Scottish universities
where the old Scots tongue, which had almost superseded Latin by
the middle of the century, was being rapidly assimilated to English.

One great advantage common to Leyden and Edinburgh, in the
opinion of the students who flocked to these seminaries, was the
absence of the strict discipline imposed by residence even in an
eighteenth-century college. Many parents were not so sure that this
was an advantage; but they thought the practical consequences of
their sons' freedom from restraint were less likely to be dangerous in
a city where social life was still under the inspection of the Kirk than
in a continental university town.

Another resemblance between Edinburgh and the continental university towns was the provision made for teaching subjects which
were not included in the curriculum of the university but were equally

necessary, according to the ideas of the time, to the education of a gentleman. There were private teachers to give instruction in modern languages, especially French, and in the arts of painting and music. The Musical Society, founded in 1728, gave concerts regularly from 1762 in Saint Cecilia's Hall in Niddries Wynd. The teacher of French usually had a room allocated to him in the College and is sometimes described in Senate minutes as 'teacher of French in this University'. Under a succession of Italian masters, and linked closely with the University, the Royal Academy gave instruction in fencing and riding.

Much importance was attached to dancing lessons, which were regarded as essential to all those whose intended profession involved constant appearances in public, whether as preachers of the Gospel, or lawyers or diplomats. And here Edinburgh enjoyed one great advantage over the other Scottish universities; it was still for many purposes a capital city. Most parents preferred that their children should attend lectures during the day, while mixing with good society in the evenings, rather than have them shut up in an Oxford college.

The few English aristocrats who came to be educated at Edinburgh nearly always boarded with the professors, who could exercise some supervision over their extra-mural activities and introduce them to Edinburgh society. A polyglot Edinburgh alumnus, Necker de Saussure, emphasised the point that at Edinburgh, while pursuing their studies, undergraduates could also acquire 'ces connoissances diverses qui peuvent en faire dans la suite des citoyens utiles et des hommes de bonne société'. The combination of many young students seeking a professional qualification with a less numerous but still appreciable number of mature non-graduating students, intent on obtaining a liberal education, was the basis of the University's success since it led the youngsters to see in their studies not a disagreeable task but an enjoyable pursuit.

Although much fewer in number than the English and Irish contingents, the overseas students must be considered separately. The bulk of them apparently came from the West Indies and the mainland colonies of North America to study medicine. This generalisation is based on the record of medical graduates; a *caveat* should perhaps be entered that, since Arts students hardly ever graduated at the end of their course, and the Arts professors did not enter the place of origin of their students in their class records, it is really impossible to give any quantitative estimate of the number of overseas students in the Arts Faculty in the eighteenth century.

It seems likely that of the Arts Chairs the Chair of Rhetoric exerted most influence upon the trend of American education in the eighteenth century. This was not primarily due to the attendance of American students at Blair's lectures, but to the interest taken in the subject by another Edinburgh alumnus, John Witherspoon, who took up appointment as president of the College of New Jersey, now better known as Princeton, in 1768. Witherspoon gave 'the first formal course in rhetoric in the American colonies'. His indebtedness in these lectures to Blair was obvious. Harvard and Yale soon followed Princeton's example, and well into the nineteenth century Blair's *Lectures on Rhetoric and Belles Lettres* was the standard text-book on the subject in American universities.*

During his eleven years as professor of Chemistry, Cullen had forty American students. Many of these sent their own promising pupils to Edinburgh in later years. Cullen gave them all a cordial welcome and became the idol of his American students.† Some of them were prigs like Benjamin Rush, who was 'determined to cultivate the acquaintance of men of learning and virtue', wherever he went.‡ All of them set store on the MD degree 'as a palpable record of accomplishment to take home with them'.§ Only about half of the American students who attended Cullen's chemistry lectures graduated at Edinburgh; others took degrees, after studying at Edinburgh, at universities with less strict residence requirements, such as Leyden, or at other Scottish universities which gave MD degrees without either teaching or examining the candidates. Most of the colonial MDs of Glasgow 'before 1800 had been trained by Edinburgh'.‖ Mr Riggs has calculated that one in nine or ten of the students who took the MD degree at Edinburgh before 1776 was an American, while many other graduates emigrated to the American colonies after their graduation.

---

* L. T. Chapin, 'American Interest in the Chair of Rhetoric and English Literature in the University of Edinburgh' in *Univ. of Edin. Journal*, xx (1961), pp. 118–20.
† W. J. Bell, 'Some American Students of "That Shining Oracle of Physic", Dr William Cullen of Edinburgh, 1755–66' in *Proceedings of the American Philosophical Society*, xciv, pp. 275–81.
‡ G. W. Corner, 'Benjamin Rush's Student Days in Edinburgh, and what came out of Them' in *Univ. of Edin. Journal*, xv, p. 127.
§ A. R. Riggs, 'The Colonial American Student at Edinburgh' in *Univ. of Edin. Journal*, xx, p. 143.
‖ Ibid., p. 143.

Benjamin Franklin remarked in 1776 that at Edinburgh 'at this time there happen to be collected a set of as truly great men, professors of the several branches of knowledge, as have ever appeared in any age or country';* and the original medical schools of the United States of America, founded at Philadelphia in 1765 and in New York in 1767, were established and at first staffed by Edinburgh graduates and deliberately modelled by them on the Edinburgh Medical School. Even during the American War of Independence, American students continued to frequent the University of Edinburgh and, in spite of growing provision in their own country for medical education on Edinburgh lines, they even increased in number in the closing years of the eighteenth and the early years of the nineteenth centuries. Between 1765 and 1865 at least 650 Americans graduated MD at Edinburgh. If the Atlantic community had been shattered politically, the influence of Edinburgh helped to preserve a common culture on both sides of the Atlantic. Even accepting that the magnet which drew nearly all of them to Edinburgh was the MD degree, many American students gained distinction in other professions than medicine. Some went into politics, including Arthur Lee, the first American ambassador to France. John Jeffries gained notoriety as a pioneer balloonist; Tucker became a poet of some repute; and William Thornton attained fame as an inventor and architect. The influence of Edinburgh in the nineteenth century upon Canadian medical schools, especially the Medical Faculty of McGill University, was as strong as it had been in the United States in the eighteenth century. Before 1867, 104 Canadian-born students had graduated MD at Edinburgh.

By no means all the 'overseas' students came from North America. Two Polish students graduated MA in 1726, and some Polish nobles in the early nineteenth century, fearing that their sons would be infected by the Romantic movement, sent them to study at Edinburgh. They included Andrzej Zamoyski, his cousin Leon Sapieha, and a son of Thomasz Lubienski.† The Princess Dashkova, who had been the intimate friend of the Russian Empress, Catherine II, brought her son Paul to Edinburgh to be educated and presented a cabinet of medals to the Senatus. A few years later, in 1786, Ignatius Maria Ruiz Luzuriaga also took the degree of MA, as did Ignazio Joseph de

---

* W. L. Sachse, *The Colonial American in Britain*, p. 56.
† R. F. Leslie, *Polish Politics and the Revolution of November, 1830*, p. 105.

Pereira in 1814. Benjamin Constant, one of the founders of French liberalism under the Restoration monarchy, spent two academic years at Edinburgh (1783–85) – a period which contributed to develop his political ideas, and which he later described as 'l'année la plus agréable de ma vie'.

A number of French *émigrés* were students at Edinburgh during the French Revolution and several took the MD degree. Madame de Staël in 1804 proposed to send her son Auguste to the University, and her young relation, L. A. Necker de Saussure, did study at Edinburgh from 1806–8. A few years later Castlereagh, as secretary of state for foreign affairs, informed Principal Baird that the Tsar and the·ex-King of Sweden proposed to send Prince Gustavus of Sweden 'to receive part of his education' at Edinburgh University. The German historian Niebuhr spent an academic year at Edinburgh, but was not greatly impressed. On the whole, Edinburgh's influence upon European scholarship and culture was exerted by the written rather than by the spoken word.

TOWN-COUNCIL PATRONAGE AND ADMINISTRATION

If it is correct to attribute the growing reputation of the University in the eighteenth century to the eminence of its professors, aided perhaps by a certain paucity of competition elsewhere, the credit must be given to the body which chose these professors, the town council. One English visitor after another* paid tribute to the 'incorruptible fidelity and sound discrimination' of the town council in electing professors, although it must be added that most of them can have had little idea of how these elections were actually conducted. Even at the time it was sometimes regarded as anomalous that an unlearned body of merchants and craftsmen who alone were eligible for membership of the council, proved so skilful on the whole in electing the best candidates to Chairs. Attempts have been made to show that the council acted on advice, usually political advice from the government party manager for Scotland or one of his assistants. Whether these party managers, left to themselves, would have been likely to do as well by the University as the town council certainly did is an open question. Sometimes the council also received unsolicited advice from the medical students, about filling Chairs and distributing teaching duties

---

* Sir John Carr, *Caledonian Sketches*, p. 94, amongst many others.

between medical professors.* In any case, whoever was consulted or offered advice, the final decision rested on a vote by the whole council.

It should also be pointed out that the Law Chairs, in which the learned Faculty of Advocates had a large share in making appointments, were certainly not filled by the best professors, presumably because the Faculty was influenced by non-academic considerations. Elections to the Humanity Chair in which the Lords of Session, advocates, and writers to the signet shared patronage with the town council, were often fiercely disputed and academic considerations usually played a very minor role. One of Charles Mackie's letters, among the Leven and Melville Papers, gives a spirited and amusing account of such an election in 1742. When Regius Chairs were founded and their patronage strictly reserved to the Crown, the town council regarded successive appointments to these Chairs as infringing their rights as patrons of the College. For centuries the College bailie solemnly presented to the Senatus for induction the man chosen by the Crown and then, with equal solemnity, recorded a protest by the town council against the appointment.

But in the great majority of cases the town council alone were the patrons; and not only were they proud of the good name of the town's College, they soon realised that the growing reputation of the University was a tangible asset to the town. Calculations began to appear as to how much profit the merchants, craftsmen, and landladies of Edinburgh made annually from the concourse of students.

In the earlier part of the eighteenth century an argument often used in favour of establishing a new Chair was that it would enable Scottish students to study at home and thus avoid expense to individuals and reduce the national requirements for foreign currency. By the second half of the century this argument had often been stood on its head and the town council hoped to bring prosperity to the town by attracting professors of reputation from elsewhere. One tourist calculated that the Edinburgh students spent in the town during a session of seven or eight months not less than £30,000.† When the town council offered a Philosophy Chair to Francis Hutcheson of Glasgow and actually brought Cullen and Black from Glasgow Chairs and Gregory from Aberdeen, some councillors were probably thinking

---

* Pamphlets in EUL Att. 80 (P4) No. 1.
† Robert Heron, *Observations made in a Journey through the Western Counties of Scotland*, II, p. 502.

not only of the intellectual gain to their University, but also of the material profits that would accrue to the town. One English visitor, Thomas Newte, perhaps overstated the case when he wrote that when able professors appeared at the other Scottish universities, 'they have generally been invited to Edinburgh, where the greatest abilities, in every branch of education, have been concentrated as in a focus'.

The seventeenth-century practice of appointing regents by competitive trials, though it had lost most of its vitality, lingered on. When Colin Drummond wished to have Robert Law joined with him as joint professor of Greek in 1738, the Senatus, at the request of the town council, appointed the principal and three professors to act as 'examinators' along with two of the Edinburgh ministers – the trial to take place in presence of the magistrates, the other masters of the College, and the other ministers of the town. The last occasion of this kind was probably on the appointment of Andrew Dalzel as assistant and successor to the professor of Greek in 1772. Several members of Senatus testified from personal knowledge to Dalzel's qualifications: nonetheless a committee of Senatus conducted a trial of 'considerable length' in which Dalzel read and explained several passages in prose and verse from Greek and Latin authors and gave such answers to questions addressed to him by members of the committee that the committee recommended his appointment. This practice would seem to have been confined to the older Chairs which dated back to the period of teaching by regents. Bower believed that Dalzel's appointment was really due to the influence of his patron, the Earl of Lauderdale, over the town council.

The powers of the town council did not stop with patronage; they extended to minute regulation of every aspect of the administration and life of the College. From the sixteenth to the nineteenth centuries the town council frequently drew up rules for the conduct of various officials of the College from the principal down to the under-janitor. Without their sanction no laws could be made for the College. They claimed, for example, in the late seventeenth century the right to regulate the system of fines which was growing up for student offences and to control the distribution of the proceeds. They objected most strenuously and persistently to any attempt by the masters of the College to organise themselves as a corporate or quasi-corporate body. While allowing perforce that the masters should conduct a preliminary examination for the degree of MA they reserved the right to fix the date of graduation and prescribe the ceremonies which should accompany it. One hundred and fifty years later they still claimed the right to make regulations for courses and examinations leading to any degree. It was the town council which allocated accommodation in the College and decided whether a professor had made out a case to have a new classroom built for him. Although by the eighteenth century professors' commissions were *aut vitam aut culpam*, an infirm professor had to apply to the town council if he wished to have an assistant and successor, or even a temporary deputy, appointed to carry out his duties. Ultimate control of the University Library was also included in the town council's competence.

While the town council was never willing to abate one iota of its legal rights to control the College, the strictness with which they were exercised in practice varied greatly from time to time. Anything which could be interpreted as a challenge to their authority by the masters was not only repressed by the council, but was followed by a period of greater strictness in enforcing closer control of all the activities of the College.

With the rise in the status of university teachers in the seventeenth century and increasing contacts with the other Scottish universities, in which the masters ruled, the Edinburgh masters began to show resentment at town council control and to organise themselves. The first clear signs of this appeared in the reign of James VII, who apparently was prepared to grant incorporation to the masters of the Edinburgh College, although he was careful to confirm explicitly the rights of the town council as patrons. From the Restoration period, if not earlier, the masters met regularly to arrange the routine of business of the College and the town council turned a blind eye to the proceedings, or, perhaps, were not even aware of them.

On 20 January 1703, during a vacancy in the principalship, the masters, styling themselves 'the Faculty of Philosophy in the University of Edinburgh', fixed the date for the annual graduation and determined that the ceremony should be a private one. To make things worse, they asserted that they were acting 'according to their undoubted right contained in the Charter of Erection and their constant uninterrupted custom in such cases'. Neither claim could possibly be substantiated and the masters were forced to recant and declare their submission to the complete control by the town council of the administrative, financial, and educational affairs of the College. Indeed, had the Lord Advocate not intervened in their favour, worse might have happened to the presumptuous masters. It was at this crisis that

Principal Carstares took office and his handling of it offers convincing proof of his statesmanship.

When the town council tried to push home its victory by minute regulation of College business and tiresome harrying of the principal and masters, Carstares told the Lord Provost that he held office on no other terms than those on which his predecessors had held it. His great reputation and tactful management soon restored the *status quo*. The masters continued to meet and regulate College business; but they no longer attempted to challenge the overriding authority of the council. When different views prevailed in faculty or *senatus academicus* or university meeting* from those held in the town council a deputation of professors sometimes waited upon the College committee or the town council. More often a reasoned statement, described as a petition or memorial by its authors, was submitted in writing to the patrons.

While the town council soon relaxed its attempts to regulate minutely the business of the University, the masters won only a solitary victory in the whole course of the eighteenth century over the patrons. This came in 1723 when the town council, in spite of legal advice from Duncan Forbes, soon to be Lord President, that their claims were well founded, abandoned their right to share in the annual election of a College commissioner to the General Assembly. This willingness to accept what was a decision by the General Assembly itself may be regarded as a mark of respect to the supreme ecclesiastical authority. It may be also that members of the town council, who returned two commissioners to each assembly as representatives of the town, felt that they were already adequately represented.

One other change in the government of the College was however established definitely in the eighteenth century. The Edinburgh ministers, who had played such a prominent part in the foundation of the College and had exercised their rights, under James VI's charter of 1582, to share in its patronage and government during the seventeenth century, ceased to be active and influential in its affairs. The virtual cessation of public graduations in Arts meant that they no longer had regular occasions for visiting the University. Their presence was still occasionally invited in the first half of the century from time to time as, for example, to witness and approve the humiliation of the

---

* All three terms are used interchangeably in the earlier part of the eighteenth century for a formal meeting of the principal and masters.

masters who had challenged in 1703 the authority of the town council, or to take part in the public trials of Robert Law as professor of Greek in 1738; but there is no suggestion that they took an active part on either occasion. Even before William Robertson became principal in 1762, they seem to have disappeared entirely from the scene; and when they reappear in the early nineteenth century it is no longer to assert claims to share in the government of the University, but merely, as interested parties, to make certain that religious tests imposed by the secular authorities upon newly appointed professors were actually enforced.

WILLIAM ROBERTSON'S PRINCIPALSHIP
AND THE NEW BUILDINGS

The thirty years during which William Robertson presided over the University perhaps represent the highest point in its history. He himself was generally regarded as the foremost historian of his generation and, as leader of the moderates, he dominated the General Assembly. The town council deferred to him. It was largely owing to his influence that the Royal Society of Edinburgh was founded in 1783 'after the model of some foreign academies which have for their object the cultivation of every branch of science, erudition, and taste'. His colleagues on the Senatus followed his lead so implicitly that no divisions are recorded at any of the meetings over which he presided as principal. The popularity of his published works spread the fame of the University beyond Europe into America and Asia. 'It was, with reason, believed abroad that the seminary of education, in which the historian of Mary, of Charles v, of Columbus, presided could not be a mean one'.* Robertson's reputation abroad increased the respect already paid to him at home as a man and an administrator. While the first principals, including Rollock, had regarded the principalship as inferior in function and dignity to the ministry, Robertson put scholarship before preaching. It was during his long tenure of office that the taking of religious tests by newly appointed professors, as prescribed by various statutes, ceased. It was not that heretics were appointed to Chairs: as long as Robertson's influence was paramount

---

* Robert Heron, *Observations made on a journey through the Western Counties of Scotland*, II, p. 497.

---

27. Principal William Robertson; detail from a painting by Sir Joshua Reynolds, *c.* 1776.

in the church and the University, formal guarantees of orthodoxy were superfluous. During his principalship, Robertson continued to preach on Sundays in one of the Edinburgh churches and as a historian he sometimes attributed the course of events to divine providence.

The impulse given by Robertson appears most clearly in the Senate minutes, which record the decisions taken by the principal and professors on University business. In the preceding years, meetings of Senatus had been rare, formal, and sparsely attended; but fifteen were held in 1763. Robertson then secured the appointment of various committees to consider and report on urgent problems. He reorganised the Library, in which he took a life-long interest, dividing it into a general branch and a medical branch. He proposed a scheme for combining all the libraries of the town in a single institution, but here he failed. By collecting half-a-crown from each student (except those in Divinity who had their own library) and persuading each of his colleagues who had not done so to make a once-for-all donation of five guineas for the purchase of books, he provided substantial funds for the University Library. He himself kept the Library accounts and saw that the money was well spent. Students were allowed to borrow a book on depositing a sum equal to its value.

Robertson revived the practice of some of his predecessors in giving a public discourse to all the students at a formal opening meeting; but this he soon abandoned. He arranged for the offer of honorary doctorates to men such as Joseph Priestley and Owen Ruffhead, editor of the *Statutes at Large*, and Lord Cardross, better known as the Earl of Buchan, who founded the Scottish Society of Antiquaries. Aware as he was of the limited financial resources of the town council, he tried to raise money for special purposes, such as the University museum, by public subscription. He appealed to the government to provide funds to increase the inadequate salaries of the old regents, now professors, of Humanity, Greek, Logic, and Natural Philosophy, whose salaries, although increased by Queen Anne, were still lower than those attached to more recently established Chairs. Although Robertson was careful to point out that his idea was not for such an increase of these salaries 'as may render [the four professors] less attentive to the instruction of their students, or independent of the emoluments arising from a diligent performance of their duty', his appeals proved in vain.

Perhaps the greatest service rendered by Robertson to the University was his contribution to securing for it new, spacious, and up-to-date buildings. Even in the seventeenth century English visitors had described the College buildings as mean; in the eighteenth century American visitors added their quota of adverse comment: Henry Marchant, for example, thought them 'a most miserable musty pile scarce fit for stables'. Bell's Wynd 'the ordinary passage to the College' from the High Street, was so full of great holes 'owing to the constant passage of brewers, their horses and slaids' that the 'coll6giners' were in danger of breaking their legs on their way to the College.

The town council naturally preferred to patch up the existing buildings, but shortly before Robertson's appointment they had been forced to carry out one major project of reconstruction. The notorious Mrs Anderson, who had taken over her husband's printing business on his death and remained University printer for many years, had been allowed by the town council to erect and run her printing presses in the lower storey of the 1642 library building, while she used the garret above the 1617 library to dry her printing papers. In 1753 the town council had decided to raise the 1617 building by thirteen and a half feet in order to provide above the existing second storey a gallery for the accommodation of books and also a more commodious garret above the gallery as a fourth storey. Once the books had been transferred to the 1617 building, thus reconstructed, the town council planned to reconstruct the 1642 building, which had been endangered by Mrs Anderson's printing presses, as a common hall and museum; but the lead roof was found to be in such a bad state of repair that the corporation decided to strip off the lead, sell it, and provide a slate roof instead.

By this time, with the rise in student numbers, certain professors were striving to get better accommodation for their classes. With Robertson's backing, Monro reached an agreement with the town council for the provision of a new Anatomy theatre to be erected in accordance with Monro's own designs. Monro undertook to pay the whole cost, estimated at £300, but was to be repaid by the town council by instalments. The department of Natural Philosophy was also demanding better accommodation, but the eighteenth-century equivalent of the Educational Policy Committee gave priority to Monro, and the Anatomy theatre was erected in 1764.* Robertson then persuaded the town council that the cheapest way to provide

---

* See for details D. B. Horn, 'The Anatomy Classrooms in the present Old College, 1725–1880' in *Univ. of Edin. Journal* (Spring 1965), pp. 65–71.

additional classroom accommodation would be to raise the roof of the semi-derelict 1642 library building in the same manner that they had already raised the roof of the 1617 library. Accordingly the lead was removed from the roof, carefully guarded by soldiers, sold, and the proceeds used as a substantial contribution to the cost of reconstructing the 1642 library and providing it with a slate roof. The new upper storey in this building was shared by the department of Natural Philosophy and the newly instituted Chair of Natural History.

By now Robertson was convinced that these piecemeal improvements were merely tinkering with the basic problem of fitting an expanding university into makeshift buildings which had been adapted to house a small college. On 4 December 1767 the Senate appointed a committee to converse with the patrons about the rebuilding of the College. By March 1768 the Senate approved the requirements for the new buildings, fourteen classrooms of varying size, some of them to be shared by two professors. Special provision was to be made for such subjects as Natural Philosophy with its experimental needs, and Natural History, which required direct access to the museum. Each professor should have 'a retiring room, adjoining as near as possible to each of their respective classes'. In addition to a common hall 80 feet by 40 feet and a Museum 90 feet by 30 feet, a new Library building would be requisite. Although the Library had been rebuilt and expanded a few years earlier, it was now 'nearly full and books are increasing fast'. Next to the Library there should be a room 20 feet square for faculty meetings and degree examinations, and 'in which the librarian should do the necessary business of the Library and receive new books'.

The town council co-operated heartily. They hired John Laurie, a qualified surveyor, to make a survey of the area of the College; and David Henderson, architect, using the information supplied by Laurie about the site and by the professors about the accommodation required, made a plan of the proposed College. While Laurie's plan, reproduced on pp. 10–11, has been discovered amongst the Clerk of Penicuik papers, I have failed to trace Henderson's work. In December 1767 the town council decided to approach individuals for subscriptions, as they had already done with some success for erecting

---

28. The two principal University buildings of the seventeenth century as reconstructed in the eighteenth before their destruction to make way for the Adam/Playfair 'Old College'; lithograph by J. Skene, 1817.

Museum, Hall, Library.

College 1817.—

the Exchange in 1754. Subscription lists would be opened simultaneously at London, during the session of Parliament, to appeal to 'Englishmen of rank and opulence connected with the University of Edinburgh' as well as at Edinburgh. The total cost of building sixteen private schools was put at £6,500, while a public hall, library, museum, chemical laboratory, anatomical theatre, and public schools could be provided for about £8,500, so that £15,000 in all would be required. According to the *Scots Magazine* the lists opened in March 1768 and considerable sums were subscribed promptly. It was, however, stated that 'no part of the subscription is to be demanded till a sum be subscribed sufficient to build the schools or teaching rooms' which were the first priority, and we must conclude that the whole subscriptions promised totalled less than £8,500.

The complete failure of his ambitious plans must have been a blow to the principal; but he continued to press the town council for piecemeal requirements and secured a new chemistry classroom and laboratory. This was erected in 1781–2 on a vacant piece of ground on the north side of the old Lower Court. There were also rumours about this time that the Crown might hand over to the town for use as a College 'the neighbouring palace of Holyrood-house, now languishing in a deserted state', presumably as an alternative to the rebuilding of the College on its original site. By this time, in any case, the further expansion of the University must have rendered obsolete Henderson's design for a new College. Professor James Gregory pointed out that most of the professors had had to apply to the town council during the twenty years since 1764 'to have their teaching rooms enlarged or new ones fitted up for them that might contain their students', who had increased four-fold in the past hundred years. Although built late in 1764 the Anatomy theatre had twice required to be altered to squeeze in more students, while the professor of Chemistry had had to teach for a time in the University museum and the professors of the practice of Physick in 'the public hall of the newly-built High School'.

The leading architect of the day, Robert Adam, was not only an Edinburgh alumnus, but the son of Robertson's full cousin, William Adam. In life the Robertsons and the Adams were linked by ties of friendship as well as of cousinhood and in death William Adam and Principal Robertson lie in adjoining lairs in Greyfriars Kirkyard. Robert Adam's design for the east front and other parts of a new college were circulating in Edinburgh by 1785 and the building of

29. Robert Adam; a medallion by James Tassie, 1792.

30. Robert Adam's design for the east front of the new University buildings.

the South Bridge, for which Adam himself had drawn up plans, meant that the College buildings, 'like so many hovels or barns irregularly put together' and formerly tucked away in an obscure corner of the town, were now exposed to the view of everyone approaching Edinburgh from the south. The town council had made over free of charge the part of the College gardens needed to construct the southern access to the South Bridge on the plea that the College would benefit by the new means of communication. They undertook also to apply any profit made by selling frontages on the new street to the rebuilding of the College. The buildings erected on these sites, including the many elegant and spacious shops which so impressed English and foreign visitors, must by contrast have made the old buildings of the College appear even more mean and contemptible.

Encouraged by Henry Dundas, an Edinburgh alumnus, MP for Edinburghshire and the uncrowned king of Scotland, the town council decided in 1789 to try once again, under more favourable conditions, the tactics which had failed in 1768. Within a few months the £15,000

which was all that had been asked for in 1768 had been subscribed.
So confident were they of public support that the town council
arranged for laying the foundation stone of the new College on 16
November 1789 at 'that part of the east front immediately on the
right as you enter the northern-most foot passage near the Great Gate'.
A few days earlier Adam had 'viewed the different houses in the New
Town to judge what stone was proprest to build the College with . . .
[and] fixed on Craigleith and Ravelstone for all ashlar and mouldings
etc.' Amid scenes of popular enthusiasm, professors in their gowns
and students in their hats, distinguished with sprigs of laurel supplied by the town council, had walked together in the procession 'in
one academical body', with the town council and a great concourse
of freemasons. 'Long, long,' they chanted to the tune of the Hero comes,

Long, long, dishonour of our Isle,
Neglected lay the Muse's pile;
Her fav'rite walls neglected lay,
Rude, mean, and mould'ring to decay.

And on the return journey, to the tune of Britannia rules the Waves,
    The stone we've seen first plac'd by Napier's hand,
    Whose future pile aloft shall rise,
    Whose fame shall spread through every distant land,
    And, raised by time, shall reach the skies.

The one discordant note came from the 'Associated Students of Medicine', who inserted an advertisement in the *Caledonian Mercury* to state that they regarded as an insult the shortness of the invitation to attend the ceremony and had therefore stayed away. The noblemen and gentlemen who attended were entertained by the corporation at the Assembly Rooms, when toasts were drunk such as 'Success to the New University' and 'A long continuance to the Old Chairs in the New College'. During the winter the masons hewed and dressed stones in an 'expensive and commodious' shed at the west end of the old Royal Infirmary and the remaining buildings on the north-east of the site were taken down. Then in February 1790 the demolition of the north-western buildings began and on 1 April 1790 the foundation stone of a new Anatomical theatre was laid on this part of the site. Partly to reduce the danger of subsidence at the north-east corner, Adam's clerk of works, John Paterson, began on the same day to dig out the foundations at the south-east corner. Professor Monro wanted and apparently secured 'subterraneous passages', presumably for the secret conveyance of subjects for dissection in the Anatomy theatre. He also wanted but did not get a pit in which the remains could be buried in quick-lime. Adam's plans show also a subterranean passage intended for bringing agricultural machines in connection with the agriculture class from a building on the north side of the present Chambers Street into the College building. One such passage is known to exist at the present day.

By July 1790 it was clear that the building costs would soon outrun subscriptions, unless new sources could be tapped. The Trustees for the new buildings now proposed to collect small sums from the inhabitants of Edinburgh and to make personal application to the noblemen and gentlemen who, from their distance from Edinburgh and for other reasons, had not yet subscribed. By 22 September 1790 £5,480 11s. 4d. had been spent on the building, roughly the amount actually paid by the subscribers, and the Trustees calculated that the rest of the money already promised would probably suffice to complete the east front and the Anatomy block at the north-west corner of the site. The *Caledonian Mercury* explained that 'though the work is

31. Detail from an engraving by David Allan of the laying of the foundation
    stone of the new University building in 1789.

executed in the most substantial manner, the utmost frugality has
been observed, much less money having been expended than could
reasonably have been expected'.

Adam and Paterson were already having trouble with a prominent
Edinburgh builder, Alexander Reid, who had originally been recommended to them by Dundas himself as the best man to carry out the
mason's work contract on the new buildings. Adam beat down Reid's
prices for the east front by getting another mason to offer to do the
work at cheaper prices. Reid reluctantly reduced his and then, after
a day's reflection, refused to proceed further with the works of the
College. Adam was thus able to employ the other mason, Crichton;
but Reid soon secured appointment as Deacon-Convener of the
Trades, which made him an *ex officio* Trustee for the College buildings
and gave him opportunities of raising difficulties which he eagerly
seized.

Nevertheless, in the summer of 1790 work went steadily on along
the whole east front as well as at the north-west corner. From October
to December 1790 Paterson was supervising the quarrying and trans-

port to the site of the first of the great Doric columns – each a monolith 24 feet in height – to adorn the main entrance, while Adam was now drawing plans for the north front of the College and the cross-building which was to separate the two quadrangles. It was at this time also that Adam was asked by the Lord Provost to design a crescent immediately to the east of the College, across South Bridge Street, 'with a concert hall in the centre of it'. By February 1791 Adam had completed his plans for the ground storey of the north front and also for the west front which was to house the graduation hall, with underneath it a room with stone piers intended to support the floor of the hall above. He also sent to Paterson a model of the roof of the College with detailed instructions about the parts to be executed in seasoned oak, or choice pieces of fir or elm, the last-named wood being selected for the ribs of the dome above the Anatomy theatre since it was 'lighter than fir, and much better to cut circular, and the difference of expense is so little that it cannot be an object worth attending to'.

Trouble with Reid came to a head in the winter of 1790–1 and was the more serious because Reid was supported by the Lord Provost and the Lord Justice Clerk, who objected to a remark attributed to Adam that 'as architect and surveyor to the University of Edinburgh' he would 'employ whom he pleased at the College and at what price he pleased'. This they contended made the Trustees a body of dummies. Fortunately this difficulty was got over and by 9 March 1791 the Lord Provost complimented Paterson 'on the rapidity of the buildings, the goodness of the work, and the measures taken to accomplish it'. By this time Paterson was erecting the columns of the east front and crowning them with capitals, a work of some technical difficulty which was closely watched not only by Lord Provost Stirling, but by his immediate predecessor, Elder. When Stirling and Gray, Clerk to the Trustees, visited Adam in London in April 1791 he found them both 'facetious and civil'. Finance was now an urgent problem and the Provost proposed to have Adam's fronts and plans engraved and sent to Jamaica 'from whence he expects handsome subscriptions'. Considerable sums had already been promised from the West as well as from the East Indies; but there seem to have been difficulties in securing payment in full from some subscribers.

Robert Adam's death in 1792 may have contributed to these difficulties, although he left behind him virtually complete plans not only for the College but also for the crescent with concert room, booksellers' *salon*, restaurant, and shops on the other side of South Bridge

Street. Probably more important was the diversion of public attention to the outbreak of war with France in 1793 and its social and economic consequences. The upper classes, whether Whig or Tory, had now to meet the demands of war taxation and were offered opportunities for investment in war loans which were equally patriotic and remunerative. The government policy of repression which followed upon the outbreak of war soon created an atmosphere quite different from that in which the University appeal had been so successfully launched. And Henry Dundas, as Pitt's right-hand man in carrying on the war, can have had little time or energy to spend upon less immediate problems. In 1789 the *Caledonian Mercury* had published verses referring to the clever chiels in Edinburgh who proposed

To rear a College,
In hopes to fill our kintry roun'
Wi' truth an' knowledge.

By 1793–4 the newspapers were preoccupied with the needs of national defence against the French Revolution and its sympathisers, open and concealed, in Britain. The preoccupation of Dundas and his friends with these new problems probably did more to cause the failure of the University appeal than the death of Robert Adam, who, after all, left behind him brothers who were also architects of repute and perfectly capable of carrying out their elder brother's plans.

Early in 1794, when lack of funds had brought building operations to an end, the east block had been more or less completed; accommodation had been provided at the north-west corner for Anatomy, Practice of Physic, and Moral Philosophy; and the central part of the western block, later to form a Natural History museum, was under construction. But a considerable part of these buildings had to be left unroofed with beams and joisting exposed to the weather, while the College area was embarrassed with sheds, stones, and other materials, and unauthorised persons were able to gain access to the quadrangle in the evenings.

No sooner had the old buildings been destroyed than regrets began to be expressed. According to Robert Heron, 'the old buildings . . . were not unsuitable to the modes of living in the country, at the time when they were erected, and certainly did honour to the taste and munificence of the citizens of Edinburgh in the days of James vi'. Although Heron went on to describe them as 'comparatively mean and smoky huts', he stated also that they had 'a venerable and dignified air by their antiquity'. In 1799 the Trustees pointed out to Henry

Dundas, now Secretary of State for War, that the unfinished parts of the new buildings were likely soon to become ruinous; but it was not until 1801 that a reluctant government provided £5,000 for 'putting the incomplete buildings of the University in a state of security as far as possible'.

SOCIAL LIFE

Not much is known of the social contacts between Edinburgh professors in the eighteenth century. We get a glimpse from Calamy's *Life and Times* of the regents inviting their revered Principal Carstares to a fish supper at Newhaven–apparently an annual event, which Calamy much enjoyed. At this time also every master, on being appointed, was expected to give a feast to his colleagues; but in 1737 the newly appointed principal, William Wishart, set the example of contributing to the Library a promissory note of £10 and 'a parcel of curious books' (one hopes that the adjective had not yet acquired its present meaning in booksellers' catalogues) 'in lieu of any entertainment usual at admissions of masters'. After this there is little evidence of social activities, unless we count Senatus attendance at funerals, until Andrew Duncan, senior, of the Theory of Medicine Chair and famous for his foundation of clubs, proposed that members of Senatus should meet in a 'Social Annual Convention'.

The first of these in March 1792 arranged for Raeburn to paint the portrait of Principal Robertson which now hangs in the Senate Hall, but the emphasis continued to be social and recreative after the rigours of the long winter session. Indeed, on one occasion, the members of Senatus are described as 'dissipated' during the short Christmas vacation, which had often been limited to three days earlier in the century, but now usually lasted just over a week so as to include both Christmas and New Year. However, it seems that the writer of this particular minute merely meant that the professors had scattered at the end of term and could not be collected for a meeting.

There is much more evidence of how students spent their spare time in the eighteenth century than there is for the seventeenth. It is true that the last attempt to bring up to date the ancient laws of the University, which was a valuable source for the earlier period, took place in 1733. New rules were prescribed in 1736 which *inter alia* prohibited students from climbing on the roofs of any College buildings or from making a disturbance while any master was teaching. From time to time the masters tried to revive the ancient practice of attendance by staff and students at divine service in the Loft of Lady Yester's Church; but they were now more concerned to exclude those who were not students from the College Loft than to ensure complete attendance of the whole student body. In any case, the number of students was much too great for them all to be accommodated and that the gallery was in fact sparsely occupied is suggested when the Senatus Academicus authorised 'a band of singers of bass' to use 'one of the square seats in the College gallery' and added that this 'would not be attended with any inconveniency to the students'.

By this time there must have been a marked cleavage between the bulk of the Scottish students, released from school in their early teens, and the more mature students from elsewhere, many of them already men of the world and much better endowed with this world's goods than the great majority of the Scots. The divinity students are often specifically mentioned for their poverty and unkempt condition; and even Topham remarked that the Scottish students were not 'so remarkable for their cleanliness and politeness as for their poverty, famine and science'. While the juvenile Scots continued to bicker with the High School boys, throw snowballs and sometimes stones at each other and the passers-by, or sneak into the half-built College after 1794 to play ball in the evenings, the older students spent much of their time in taverns, frequented the playhouse in the winter and made up parties of pleasure in the summer to visit the surrounding country. Penicuik was a favourite place of resort. It was famous for its strawberries and there were two roads to it so that a round tour was easy to arrange. Golf was enjoyed or at least played on Leith Links and at Musselburgh. There were several bowling greens in the neighbourhood of the College to which students resorted. Skating was a popular pastime in winter, riding and going to the races in the summer. There is occasional mention of bathing in the sea. By way of indoor recreation, billiards, although frowned upon by the authorities, was still often played. As late as 1790, all the keepers of billiard tables in the town were convened before the magistrates and fined and their tables ordered to be destroyed, on the ground that resort to billiard rooms tended to pervert the morals of youth.

Dances and concerts were regularly held under distinguished patronage at the Assembly Rooms, St Cecilia's Hall, and elsewhere.*

---

* A full and contemporary account of the games played in eighteenth-century Edinburgh will be found in *Anecdotes & Egotisms of Henry Mackenzie*, ed. H. W. Thompson, pp. 74–90.

According to the *Caledonian Mercury*, during the first week of August 1789 thirty-one 'public amusements' were available in Edinburgh, besides many others of inferior note. On one occasion, at least, Adam Smith took a foreign scholar to hear a competition on the bagpipes.* The more earnest students spent part of their spare time with private tutors, studying modern foreign languages, music or drawing, or writing verses which occasionally found a publisher. Boon companions were liable to quarrel with each other in their cups and pursue their quarrels in the streets. On two or three occasions pistols were flourished or even fired in the classrooms; now and again such quarrels ended in formal duels. At other times the Senatus interposed its authority to keep order: any student who gave or accepted a challenge was liable to be expelled. Henry Brougham, later to be Lord Chancellor, described how he spent his evenings as a student at Edinburgh with a gang of his friends whose principal delight was in wrenching off the brass knockers on the doors of the houses in the New Town. Such escapades, especially when repeated, sometimes led to students appearing in the Burgh Court. In view of the peculiar relationship between the University and the town there could be no problem, such as existed elsewhere, of conflict of jurisdictions between town and gown.

By this time student societies were a well-established feature of the Edinburgh scene. As early as 1720 a society for students interested in natural philosophy is mentioned and its 'collection of books relating to physical science' was, on its demise, bequeathed to the University Library. Principal Robertson as a student was a prominent member of one such society and after he became principal he encouraged the formation of student clubs. University societies usually began as private debating clubs of students interested in a particular branch of study, as was the case with the Royal Medical Society, the oldest surviving organisation of its kind. Others were primarily dining clubs and some of these were intended to promote social contacts between, for example, American or Irish medical students. Some clubs, notably the Royal Medical and the Royal Physical Societies, had sufficient resources to obtain charters from George III and to build their own halls. Most of the early societies met in taverns. The Speculative Society, on the other hand, although its members were not all Edinburgh alumni, was allowed to hold its meetings in a special room set apart for the purpose in the old Old College, and was allocated another room in

---

* B. Faujas de St Fond, *Travels* (Engl. Translation), ii, p. 242.

the new buildings. Although the theological students had their own society from 1776, the earliest specific society of law students is the Scots Law Society, founded in 1815.

It would be difficult to overestimate the importance of these student societies in the life of the eighteenth-century university. They did something to give coherence to the amorphous Edinburgh undergraduate body and provided opportunities both for debate and relaxation which were badly needed. Many of the ablest students, and others who were not so able, have placed on record their debts to such societies. Charles Townshend, one of the best speakers in the House of Commons, at a time when it was famous for its oratory, was so intimidated by the Select Society that he was unable to address it effectively.* Judging by what students so diverse as Brougham, Benjamin Constant, and Necker de Saussure wrote in after life of their student days at Edinburgh, it is quite clear that they learned as much from these student societies as from the professors in the classrooms. If the University of Edinburgh still continued to be *par excellence* the university which prepared young men for active and useful careers, this was no longer due solely to the width of its curriculum and the manner in which the component subjects were taught by its professors.

The great majority of the professors as also of the students who did not live with their families or their relations, wherever these happened to be established in or around Edinburgh, usually clustered closely around the College buildings. The principal, librarian, and professors of Divinity, Greek, and Hebrew had houses in the College itself. Bristo, Lothian Street, the two College Streets, one to the north and the other to the south of the Old College, and the High Street were thickly populated by students, although we occasionally hear of students who lodged in distant suburbs.

When the South Bridge was being built, James Craig, the original projector of the New Town, put forward a scheme for two crescents, one running south-eastwards and the other south-westwards from the south end of the new bridge, enclosing between them a wide open space with views across it to the College precinct and the old Royal Infirmary. The professors, as well as doctors and surgeons connected with the Infirmary, would occupy many of the houses in this university crescent, while the rest would be available to accommodate students. Needless to say, no steps were taken to turn this town

---

* *The Anecdotes and Egotisms of Henry Mackenzie*, ed. H. W. Thompson, p. 40.

planner's dream of a *cité universitaire* from blueprint to reality. A great opportunity was thereby lost; and it is only since the last war, when the University authorities took up and vigorously pursued the George Square development that plans for a university quarter again became a live issue in Edinburgh.

Perhaps the best general appreciation of the University of Edinburgh in this period was written by Sir James Mackintosh, himself an alumnus, in an autobiographical fragment:

> I am not ignorant of what Edinburgh then was. I may truly say, that it is not easy to conceive a university where industry was more general, where reading was more fashionable, where indolence and ignorance were more disreputable. Every mind was in a state of fermentation. The direction of mental activity will not indeed be universally approved. It certainly was very much, though not exclusively, pointed towards metaphysical inquiries. Accurate and applicable knowledge were deserted for speculations not susceptible of certainty, nor of any immediate reference to the purposes of life. Strength was exhausted in vain leaps, to catch what is too high for our reach. Youth, the season of humble diligence, was often wasted in vast and fruitless projects. Speculators could not remain submissive learners. Those who will learn, must for a time trust their teachers, and believe in their superiority. But they who too early think for themselves, must sometimes think themselves wiser than their master, from whom they can no longer gain anything valuable. Docility is thus often extinguished, when education is scarcely begun. It is vain to deny the reality of these inconveniences, and of other most serious dangers to the individual and to the community, from a speculative tendency (above all) too early impressed on the minds of youth.*

---

* *Memoirs of the Life of the Rt. Hon. Sir James Mackintosh*, ed. R. J. Mackintosh (London, 1835), Vol. I, pp. 29–30.

(*3*)

The Last Days of the
Tounis College

THE FRENCH Revolutionary and Napoleonic Wars influenced directly and indirectly the development of the University of Edinburgh. Since England was largely cut off from the Continent for a generation, many English tourists who would normally have spent their holidays abroad poured into Scotland and came to know the Scottish universities at first hand. The habit of sending their sons on a grand tour of Europe, which by this time had virtually superseded the older idea of educating them at a foreign university of repute, was compulsorily interrupted and never revived. This for a time increased the already considerable influx of English students to Edinburgh.

At the same time, the war led to an unprecedented demand for technical experts of all kinds and especially for artillery officers, engineers, doctors, and surgeons. Candidates for such government employment crowded out the appropriate classes in the University and this helps to explain why the number of students at Edinburgh almost doubled during these wars. To relieve pressure and provide more effective technical training, the government overrode the opposition of the existing professors to the establishment of competing Chairs. In rapid succession Regius Chairs in Clinical Surgery, Military Surgery, and Forensic Medicine were endowed by the Crown during the opening years of the nineteenth century. The first professor of Clinical Surgery, James Russell, was in the anomalous position of having no surgical cases of his own, but prelected to his students on the cases of the Royal Infirmary surgeons. In spite of its title, the Chair of Military Surgery included in its scope the prevention as well as cure of all diseases to which an army is particularly subject, military hospitals, the transportation of sick and wounded, and tropical hygiene. Just when the need for such studies had been convincingly demonstrated by the Crimean War, the government abolished the Chair in 1856. The third of these new Chairs, Forensic Medicine, was for a time the only establishment of the kind in Britain. With the notable exception of the Chair of Pathology, founded in 1831, these three new Chairs virtually completed the medical establishment as it existed to the end of the nineteenth century. The foundation of Chairs in Surgery was soon followed by the building of a Surgical hospital which was opened in 1832 in the old High School. It was presumably partly owing to the role of the University during the war and to the services rendered by Edinburgh graduates to naval and military hygiene earlier in the eighteenth century that the government, as soon as the war ended, also made provision to house such a useful institution in more appropriate buildings.

Proposals to establish Chairs in Celtic Literature and Antiquities (1807), and in Intellectual Power (1823) both failed, with the result that in Arts no new Chair was founded between 1760 and 1862. All the more important, therefore, in this faculty was the broadening and diversification of courses of instruction already available. This took different forms. Sometimes a professor would rearrange his course, or even institute an entirely distinct course, in order to cover more systematically the subjects included in his commission. Pillans in 1822 proposed to start a third Humanity class for advanced students; and in the same year Leslie wished to give, in alternate sessions, a course of special physics with the object of enabling students who had already attended his course in 'general physical science' to follow a complete course of physics over three years. There was a change in the approach to Botany under Robert Graham, first president of the

Botanical Society (1836), during whose tenure of this Chair the Physic Garden was not only removed in 1822 to its present site but came to be called the Botanic Garden. In 1823 Wallace proposed to substitute for a course on the calculus one on Astronomy and claimed that his predecessor in the Chair of Mathematics had taught Astronomy, Geography, Navigation, Gunnery, and Fortifications as well as Mathematics. A few years later Wilson, of the Moral Philosophy Chair, proposed to give winter session lectures on Political Economy. Similar developments took place in other courses. For example, Hope in 1823 introduced what proved a popular laboratory course in Chemistry and Pharmacy, which was conducted by his assistant.

Such proposals unfortunately led usually to fierce conflict in the Senatus, but changes were in fact made from time to time. Offers were sometimes received from outsiders to teach subjects not already included in the Arts curriculum, such as Drawing and French, but these were unhesitatingly rejected by the professors, inspired by self-interest and averse to competition. On the other hand, quite a number of the professors engaged on what would now be called adult education courses, usually given in the College. Some of them attracted large audiences of both sexes; and conservatives disapproved of the presence of these ladies in the College precinct, although the practice of the Anderson Institution in Glasgow could be quoted as a precedent. When Principal Lee, in 1856, called the attention of the Senatus to an advertisement 'under sanction of the patrons' of a class for 'female students' to be held in the College, he was probably more concerned with the abuse of its authority by the town council than with the presence in the quadrangle of the female students. At other times the town council expressed fears that the holding of popular courses in the College buildings by the professors, might be detrimental 'to the dignity and respectability of the University'.

In Theology, the foundation in 1846 of the Chair of Biblical Criticism filled a centuries' old gap in the Divinity school and the professor of Oriental Languages began to take his responsibility for languages other than Hebrew more seriously. In 1849 he offered to teach Hindustani during the summer session and in 1853 he added to his repertoire Persian and Arabic and, in the following year, Sanskrit. In Law, on the initiative of the Society of Writers to the Signet, the Chair of Conveyancing was established in 1825; and in what was to become the Faculty of Science a short-lived Chair of Technology existed from 1855 to 1859.

On the whole there is little indication of any great change in the character of the lecture courses given in the College by the professors to regular or public students. When a professor fell ill and could not give his own lectures, on at least one occasion, in 1820, the Senatus allowed his lectures to be read by a gentleman 'who was well acquainted with [the professor's] handwriting'. This suggests that in some departments lectures were still literally 'dictates'. Interesting in another way is the resolution of the Senatus in 1855 that no classes should meet on Wednesday after two o'clock, with the avowed object of providing time for student recreations. It seems doubtful whether this resolution would be enforced in practice at the time; but it provides a precedent for later adoption and enforcement of this rule, although even now with some exceptions.

Another change of major importance, primarily affecting the Faculty of Arts, must be mentioned. In the new buildings the University Library possessed for a time accommodation and staff adequate for its needs.* Long before he made his often-quoted remark about the true university being a library, Thomas Carlyle was taking advantage of the new facilities and the new rules about borrowing to educate himself in a way that would have been impossible to an eighteenth-century student. This applied almost as much to the Medical as to the Arts students, but in Medicine the accent was naturally on professional text-books. The final loss by the University Library of its privileges under the Copyright Act in 1837 was not an unmixed disaster. The annual sum payable by the government to compensate the University for losing its right to a free copy of any book published in Britain was used to purchase scholarly and especially foreign books. Unfortunately continuing inflation for over a century has now reduced to insignificance the government annuity received as compensation.

Some reduction in the student population was only to be expected after 1815 and should not, in itself, be regarded as a symptom of a decline in the strength and reputation of the University. A Committee of Senatus in 1840 attributed the decline in the number of students in the various faculties to the following causes: 'Every profession is overstocked. There is not the same demand for the services of educated men as in former times. Schools, academies, colleges, have started up in every corner of the land, all holding out great professions and all

---

* *Infra*, Chapter 3, p. 125.

32. Charles Darwin's matriculation card, which, at that time, also gave library privileges.

vying with each other in the liberality of their views. Old establishments cannot afford to run the same race of popularity, and when they have attempted it, it has been at the expense of their dignity and usefulness'. While much of this must be dismissed as special pleading. the reference to increasing competition was certainly justified. Twenty years earlier a foreign visitor who was favourably impressed by the University and did not know 'any town where it would be pleasanter to live', yet put his finger on the weak spot in Edinburgh University's position: 'Edinburgh', he wrote, 'is the Birmingham of literature, a new place, which has its fortune to make. The two great universities, Oxford and Cambridge repose themselves under the shade of their laurels, while Edinburgh cultivates hers'.*

* L. Simond, *Journal of a Tour and Residence in Great Britain*, I, pp. 375–6.

At the very time when this was written, Oxford was beginning to stir from her eighteenth-century slumbers. Cambridge, whose slumbers had been rather less profound, was soon to follow the example of her older sister. Within a generation both universities had been so far reformed and revitalised that they had become fully competitive with Edinburgh in providing an education suitable for the middle classes in a modern world with constantly expanding opportunities at home and abroad. By 1855 Blackie could assert that the ancient English universities provided an education 'not only of the highest grade in certain favoured departments but more wide, broad, and free in all departments than anything that the best provided Scotch curriculum presents'. And they soon proved that they could discharge this new function without impairing in any way their older role of catering for the sons of the English aristocracy. Indeed association with the aristocrats, with its obvious value in later professional and social life, was a powerful magnet in drawing middle-class English and also aristocratic Scottish students to the English universities. In any case the academic resources of Oxford and Cambridge were so overwhelming that they had only to be properly utilised in order to restore their supremacy. How far Oxford and Cambridge reformers were influenced by the example of Edinburgh is a subject which might well be explored.

What is certain is that the new universities and colleges which in the nineteenth century came into existence in England owed much to Scotland and particularly to Edinburgh. Two Edinburgh alumni, Brougham and Mackintosh, were foremost amongst the founders of the University of London. They were joined as members of the Education Committee by five other alumni, Birkbeck, James Mill, Lord Lansdowne, Lord Dudley and Ward, and the poet Thomas Campbell, who, although more closely associated with Glasgow, had also studied at Edinburgh for a short time. Thus seven out of ten members of this Committee had been students at the University of Edinburgh. Cox, first librarian of the college, and the first Warden, Horner, were also Edinburgh men as were at least three of the first batch of professors to be appointed.

More important than *personnel* was the debt of the new institution to the Edinburgh system. As Professor Bellot puts it 'the extended range of the subjects of University study, the lecture system, the non-residence of the students, their admission to single courses, the absence of religious tests, the dependence of the professors upon fees and the democratic character of the institution, were all deliberate imitations of Scottish practice'.* A more recent commentator would seem to be well justified in his statement: 'In its shaping, London University has the appearance of a new Edinburgh, an educational new Jerusalem let down from the North'.† When all the peculiar advantages of a Scottish university education could be enjoyed in England, combined with residence in a real capital city, the flood of English students to Edinburgh inevitably dwindled, although it never entirely ceased.

In Ireland also, similar tendencies were at work in the first half of the nineteenth century. Trinity College, Dublin, had never quite sunk into the torpor of the English universities and gained strength as the new century went on. More important, London, at a time when it refused to make any substantial contribution to the finances of the Scottish universities, founded and, as it seemed to the Scots, lavishly endowed colleges for the education of Irish Roman Catholics. Though many American students still made a medical pilgrimage to Edinburgh, most of them found what they required in the medical schools of their own country, and those who completed their medical studies abroad usually preferred Paris to Edinburgh.

After the early years of the century few foreign students from the European continent were to be found at Edinburgh. The growing force of nationalisn reduced the attraction of foreign universities for students from other countries; and during and after the wars, new universities, such as Berlin, had been founded and soon attracted to themselves scholars who, under eighteenth-century conditions, might have been tempted to study abroad. The complete disappearance of Latin as the language of instruction at European universities incidentally made much more effective a barrier to international academic mobility which had come into existence during the eighteenth century.

If the French wars had indirectly increased for a time the numbers of Edinburgh students, the inflation associated with wars weakened the never strong financial position of the University. To counter this as far as possible, the matriculation fee was doubled in 1806, since the eighteenth-century fee was in the opinion of the Senatus 'too small in the present times for the purchase of books to the Library'. The fixed salaries of the professors became more and more insufficient and in 1808 the Senatus proposed that class fees, whether of two or three guineas, should all be increased by one guinea.

---

* *University College London*, p. 8.
† Chester W. New, *Life of Henry Brougham to 1830*, p. 375.

By this time the government was looking around for additional sources of revenue and in 1808 taxation was proposed upon the matriculation and graduation of students at British universities. It was in this connection that the King's Deputy Remembrancer demanded in 1810 a return of the number of students attending each professor's class. Matriculation now became compulsory and professors were forbidden to enrol students who could not produce a matriculation card. Yet, the clerk to the Senate believed that, in the session 1811–12, when 1,468 students had in fact matriculated, over 1,800 had been attending classes. In 1810 also, the Collector of Assessed Taxes was trying to collect male servant's duty in respect of all the servants employed by the professors to open their class doors. Long after the war was over, medical graduates were still paying a heavy tax to the government for their diplomas. This was felt to be even more grievous when graduates of new institutions, such as the University of London and the Queen's University of Ireland, which did not exist when the tax was first imposed, escaped payment altogether. Each Edinburgh MD paid £10 stamp duty on his diploma and, in spite of the efforts of the MP for Edinburgh, the historian Macaulay, this duty continued to be levied.

It was unfortunate for the University that in this difficult period the Senate was hampered by the lack of weight, not to say incompetence, of its principal, George Husband Baird, whose only qualification for the office was that he had married Isabella Elder, daughter of Lord Provost Elder. Baird held office from 1793 to 1840, although latterly he often failed to preside over Senate meetings and died a bankrupt. The best that his friend and colleague Sir Robert Christison could say of him was that he owed his popularity in Edinburgh society to his 'kindliness, benignant features, cheerful deportment, deferential manners, conversational power, and a rich fund of anecdote'.

Baird's successor, John Lee, who held office from 1840 to 1859, was a man of very different type. A scholar but no recluse, he had studied at Edinburgh for ten years, completing the normal courses in Arts, Medicine, and Divinity, and, according to current gossip, writing in elegant Latin many MD theses as well as his own. But Lee, the last of the clerical principals, was neither a Carstares nor a Robertson. Indeed it may be doubted whether by 1840 even a Carstares or a Robertson could have solved the questions raised by the quarrel with the town council and the resulting deadlock on reforms both in Arts and Medicine. It is hard to see that Lee exercised much influence on

FRIENDSHIP.

A principal Beard.

THE ELDER SHALL SERVE THE YOUNGER

Rom. ix. and 12.

33. Kay's satirical comment on the appointment of Professor George Husband Baird as principal by his father-in-law, Lord Provost Elder; from Kay's *Old Edinburgh Portraits*, 1793.

34. Principal John Lee; from *Modern Athenians*, drawn and etched by Benjamin Crombie, 1847.

the course of events. Occasionally he entered formal protests against decisions taken by the Crown, his colleagues, or by the town council, but in the main he seems simply to have gone along with the majority of his colleagues.

When first appointed, he had helped to restore some of the laudable customs which had been almost forgotten under his predecessor. He delivered a long series of annual addresses to students at the beginning of the session which prove the precision and elegance of his scholarship rather than its range. He tried to revive the practice of regular attendance at the Sunday services at Lady Yester's. He encouraged Divinity students to take the degree of B D and, after the Disruption, served as professor of Divinity as well as principal. It was presumably in this capacity that he persuaded the Senate that Mathematics ought to be a necessary subject for admission to the Divinity course. As befitted the leading book collector of his day in Scotland, he took a personal interest in the affairs of the Library. We may perhaps see his hand also in the petition by the Senate against the foundation of Trinity College (Glenalmond), partly on the ground that it was an institution 'founded by certain episcopalians calling themselves bishops, deans, and other ecclesiastical titles not known to the law of Scotland'. Perhaps influenced by the bankruptcy of his predecessor, he became a notable pluralist with a total emolument of about £1,300 a year. That he discharged assiduously the duties attached to these offices must serve as his excuse for publishing little beyond sermons and occasional addresses. Some of the latter prove his interest in and grasp of the history of the University and make one regret that he did not publish in a comprehensive treatise the results of his researches.

THE FACULTY OF MEDICINE AND ITS CRITICS

While there had always been disgruntled students at Edinburgh as at other universities, criticism of the system, as distinct from unfavourable comment on individual professors, is rare until the very end of the eighteenth century and then it mainly concerns the Medical Faculty. Thomas Newte in *Prospects and Observations of a Tour in England and Scotland*, published in 1791, thought the period of study required for an Edinburgh M D was too short. Students could qualify as doctors before their beards were fully grown; but he admitted that most Edinburgh medical graduates had studied Medicine elsewhere before

coming to Edinburgh. John Bristed, whose *Pedestrian Tour* was published in 1803, claimed to 'have spent two years of the most pure and
unalloyed felicity, which can, perhaps, fall to the lot of human nature,
and in the calm, the hallowed retreats of this justly distinguished and
deservedly honoured University'. But he also 'turned a look of pity
towards Edinburgh, and sighed over the fallen condition and lamented
the decaying state of the medical school'.

Bristed objected particularly to the use of Latin in medical examinations and claimed that the grinders or medical coaches 'who teach
students the jargon required for degree examinations, also sell theses
suitable for presentation by candidates'. He objected also to the vivi-
section of animals by Dr Monro *secundus* and thought that students at
English and Irish universities received 'a much more liberal and
extensive education than falls to the lot of the Scottish medical students'.
His comments must be largely discounted by his own confession that
he was a follower of Cullen's old adversary, John Brown. While other
universities, by adopting the Brunonian system, were reducing
Medicine to a 'philosophical science', Edinburgh was 'degrading it
to a mechanical and a dirty trade'.

Sir John Carr, whose *Caledonian Sketches* were published in 1807,
held that owing to difficulties in getting sufficient corpses for dissection at Edinburgh, London was 'infinitely superior' as a school of
practical anatomy, but on the contrary 'as a school of general literature
the university [of Edinburgh] ranks higher than any other'. Carr's
strictures on the teaching of Anatomy are confirmed by the efforts
made by the University deputation which visited London in 1820 to
get a better supply of corpses for dissection and by petitions from the
Senatus to both houses of Parliament on the same subject in 1828.

A more authoritative, if not better informed, criticism of the medical
curriculum was presented to the Senatus by the Faculty of Arts in
1824. Objection was taken to the grinders 'who are understood to
furnish [medical students] both with the language in which answers
to questions must be made, and with theses either written entirely
with their own hands, or corrected to such an extent as to prove the
inability of the candidates to prepare them so as to pass the revision
of the medical professors'. While the Faculty did not object to degree
examinations being conducted in English, they suggested that every
medical student should be required to produce certificates from the
appropriate Arts professors testifying to his competent knowledge of
Latin and Greek. Moreover Logic was 'absolutely necessary for a

well-informed and useful physician'. The Arts Faculty felt that 'the physician has sunk in the scale of general estimation, while the surgeon has risen to his level'. To restore the differential, would-be physicians should take Latin, Greek, Logic, and Mathematics in a two-year Arts course, followed by a three-year medical course, which should include Natural Philosophy and Natural History as well as the required medical classes.

The transparent self-interest of the Arts professors in grinding their own axes should not blind us to the defects which they proposed to cure. That there was a need for reforms was readily admitted by most of the Medical professors themselves and a good deal of the Senate's business at this time consisted of proposals for changes in the *statuta solennia*. In 1824 residence requirements were extended and regulations to secure their observance tightened up. A minimum age for beginning the course was laid down. Arts graduates were at one time amongst the privileged categories who were allowed to graduate in Medicine at the end of three instead of the normal four years study of Medicine. One Medical professor argued that to abolish the use of Latin as the language of examination would 'open a door for the graduation ... of illiterate and impudent empyricks'. Latin was thus retained for examinations and theses, but the proferred help of the Faculty of Arts in testing the candidates' knowledge was tacitly rejected.

The Statutes were however again revised by the Senatus and approved by the town council in 1832–3. In this version, the privileges extended to Arts graduates in 1824 were deleted. On the other hand while Latin was no longer used as the language of examination, all candidates must prove, by showing knowledge of classical authors, that they were 'well acquainted with Latin'. Medical theses could be written either in Latin or in English at the candidates' option. Candidates could also submit evidence, if they so desired, of their studies in 'literature and philosophy' as well as in Medicine. In the discussions of 1833 the Arts professors, again vainly, tried to write into the medical curriculum their own subjects, either in the form of a preliminary examination in Latin, Greek, Mathematics, and Philosophy or else as part of a new degree (higher than the MD) to be entitled 'a degree in Philosophy and Medicine'. It was felt that a degree which combined the two branches of study for which the University of Edinburgh had long been famous would be attractive and might strengthen its position in an increasingly competitive academic world.

Part of the trouble was simply that the holders of Medical Chairs in the early nineteenth century were, on average, much inferior to their eighteenth-century predecessors. Between 1786 and 1807 ten appointments to Medical Chairs were made and in eight of these the son of an Edinburgh Medical professor was elected. Inbreeding and nepotism could no further go. Most of these appointments were not in themselves bad. If the new professors no longer spent much time in advancing the frontiers of medical and scientific knowledge, they were usually competent lecturers. They were, however, busy practitioners and put their patients first. One of the best of them, James Gregory, explained to the Senatus in 1819 that, during his tenure of a Chair he had often been called out of town to attend patients at a great distance from Edinburgh, with the result that his 'academical lectures have been interrupted for several days, nay even for weeks together'. Although he tried to make up for lost time by lecturing six days a week 'this expedient is inadequate and precarious'. It may be for this reason that for a long time the Medical Faculty did not observe the Yule vacance or Christmas week (as it was coming to be called), customary in other faculties.

The more closely knit a university circle becomes, the greater the tension and the more bitter and frequent the internecine quarrels. This was certainly true of the Edinburgh Medical School. The class-fee system of payment encouraged professional competition and quarrels. Any attempt to found a new Chair or redistribute teaching or examining duties led to protests and often to bitter personal quarrels. Amongst the most pugnacious of the Medical professors were the two Hamiltons, who held in succession the Midwifery Chair. Their class, although well attended, was not compulsory, as were most of the other medical courses. The resulting feeling of inferiority combined with their outspoken criticisms of other Medical professors, led them into a series of lawsuits with their colleagues. As early as 1792 they were believed to have collaborated in publishing a virulent attack on other Medical professors, which led to protracted wrangles in the Senate and to James Gregory's beating the elder Hamilton with his walking-stick. When Hamilton was awarded £100 damages by the courts, Gregory remarked he would gladly pay double if he could do it again. The younger Hamilton, by appealing successfully to the town council to alter the status of the Midwifery class and thereby increase his share of tuition and examination fees, brought about the quarrel with the town council, which was to occupy the principal attention not only of the Medical Faculty but of the whole University for over thirty years.

Another sign of decline of the Medical School was the rapid development of extra-mural teaching of the basic subjects, especially Anatomy. Alexander Monro *tertius* has been accused of continuing during his tenure of the Chair to read his grandfather's lectures *verbatim*. Even an annual shower of peas from his students, we are assured, did not persuade him to alter the dates in such remarks as 'When I was a student at Leyden in 1719'. Although this story is not authentic the fact that it was generally accepted is indicative of the decline in reputation of the University school of Anatomy.* Also significant of the third Monro's attitude to his subject was his reference, in a formal return submitted to Senatus, to 'the very great and daily increasing expense of procuring human bodies and those of other animals' for dissections.

With the developing art of Surgery, there had come a change in the prevalent attitude towards Anatomy. What was wanted was no longer the academic, systematic approach of the Monros, but the supply of information needed by the practising surgeon. This was provided from about 1790 to 1804 by two brilliant extra-mural teachers, the brothers John and Charles Bell. Both ultimately were forced to desist by the University Medical professors; but John Barclay took over their class in 1804 and lectured twice daily, since his classroom could not accommodate at one sitting the hundreds of students who wished to attend.

Barclay was followed in 1824 by Robert Knox, who is mainly remembered now for his connection with the murderers, Burke and Hare, who sold to him the corpses of their victims. Though Knox himself probably did not know how the bodies had been procured, his career as an anatomist came to a premature end. Bower, in his guide to the University, printed a catalogue of extra-mural lectures given at Edinburgh in the 1820s, which occupied five pages of the guide and included one or more courses in practically all the medical subjects taught at the University. Indeed one lecturer advertised Latin lectures on Medicine and George Combe a course on Phrenology. In the 1830s and 1840s it was the extra-mural teachers who 'did more to develop surgery and to increase the fame of the Edinburgh School' than the professors. About the middle of the century

---

* See R. E. Wright-St Clair, *Doctors Monro* (London, 1964), pp. 115–17.

the extra-mural teachers of Medicine were particularly strong and
numerous. Nevertheless, it was probably the work of Goodsir
(Anatomy, 1846–67) on cellular structure which exercised the most
fundamental influence upon the development of Medicine at this
time.

One thing alarmed the Medical professors even more than competition from extra-mural teachers. This was the transformation of
medical education in England between 1830 and 1858.

During these years more fundamental changes took place in
medical education in this country than any that had occurred
before or have occurred since. The modern structure of medical
education emerged. The London and provincial medical schools
were established: the ancient libraries of Oxford and Cambridge
and the apothecary's daily round gave way to the teaching
hospital as the training ground of medical students. University
education for general practice was provided for the first time in
England by the foundation of University College London in
1826. The old-established licensing authorities began to issue
detailed syllabuses and to institute effective qualifying examinations. In 1858 the Medical Act created the General Council
for Medical Education and Registration with the task of supervising and co-ordinating medical education throughout the
United Kingdom. By the same Act regional licences were
abolished; henceforth a registered qualification was operative in
any part of the country. A register of all qualified practitioners
was compiled and all whose names appeared in it were accorded
the same legal status. Thus ended the rigid hierarchical division
of the profession into three estates, physicians, surgeons, and
apothecaries. The period 1830 to 1858 thus saw the systematiza-
tion and rationalization of medical education in England.*

The danger to Edinburgh of these changes was not merely that
students would be attracted to new or reorganised institutions which
were at last becoming fully competitive. There was an even more
serious danger. Government, under increasing pressure from new
and powerful interests elsewhere, might insist on changes in the
recognised curriculum, which would benefit rival institutions and

---

* S. W. F. Holloway, 'Medical Education in England, 1830–1858' in 49
History (1964), pp. 299–324. Mr Holloway concludes that 'medical knowledge became more scientific, medical education more systematic, and the
medical profession more unified'.

damage Edinburgh, or even exclude Edinburgh medical graduates from exercising their profession throughout the British Empire on equal terms with those of other medical schools. In 1835 the Senate sent a memorial to Lord Melbourne in which, while approving in principle the establishment in London of a metropolitan university, they protested vigorously against the proposal to grant to its medical graduates 'important exclusive privileges of practice' and to limit admission to it for purposes of graduation to students who had been taught by 'the teachers of certain corporate establishments in the metropolis'.

The Apothecaries Act of 1815 had already barred from practice as an apothecary in England any person not licensed by the London Company of Apothecaries. Since the denomination of apothecary included nine-tenths of the country practitioners in England and it was only in the large towns, if at all, that the different departments of the physician, surgeon, and apothecary were kept separate, the Act really conferred upon the Apothecaries' Company 'the monopoly of Licensing all the general practitioners in England and Wales'. In practice a nominal apprenticeship of five years and an actual residence of six or eight months in London was required by the Company, which used its monopoly to license 'a class of persons of very inferior education' and to exclude the graduates of the Universities of Edinburgh and Glasgow. Hardly less objectionable were the privileges claimed and long exercised by the London colleges of physicians and surgeons. These included monopolistic rights to practise and in 1853 Sir Robert Christison called the attention of Senatus to a clause in the charter of the London College of Physicians which authorised its fellows to take the title of MD.

Another difficulty was that government was by now prescribing minimum professional qualifications for certain categories of appointments in its own service. A degree or diploma in Surgery might be prescribed, as it was by the Poor Law Commissioners in 1842 for medical appointments under the Board, and when the Edinburgh Medical School claimed that all its doctors of medicine were fully qualified also in surgery they received from the Attorney General the unanswerable reply that what the Poor Law Reform Act of 1834 required was not proof of surgical education but the possession of a degree or diploma in surgery from a recognised institution. It was for this reason that as early as 1839 a committee of the Senatus recommended that the University should exercise its legal right to grant degrees in surgery as well as in medicine. This proposal, however, raised difficulties with the (Edinburgh) Royal College of Surgeons which were unsurmountable as long as the town council continued to govern the University. A similar problem had arisen as early as 1825 in connection with an Irish Prisons Bill.

In a very able letter to the Lord Provost, Professor James Syme pointed out some of the difficulties and deficiencies of the Medical School in 1840. The number of students was declining and, if this continued, the professors would no longer enjoy adequate remuneration nor be stimulated to exert themselves as teachers. Looked at nationally, the number of medical students had declined; but certain medical schools had actually increased their enrolment. The schools which were prosperous were the teaching hospitals of London and Dublin; and since they were not part of a university their students could not count the time spent there as qualifying for the Edinburgh MD. The strictness of the Edinburgh residence qualification for the MD also forced experienced Scottish practitioners, who wished to take the degree while continuing to practise, to have recourse to Glasgow or St Andrews. Finally, Syme, who was supported by most of his medical colleagues, argued that, in general, professors were not always the best teachers of their subjects, and especially that 'the vigour of youth and the impulse of talent may raise lecturers having no authority except what is derived from their own success to the confidence of students and the respect of the public'. Refusal to recognise these extra-mural teachers was of benefit only to lazy and inefficient professors—their abler colleagues would compete successfully on level terms and, in the absence of retiring allowances for professors, be encouraged to exert themselves 'to make provision for the evening of [their] days'. The existing system Syme concluded 'cannot be considered beneficial either for the students or for the professors'.

Syme's opponents on the Senate objected on principle to any recognition of extra-mural courses not given as part of a University programme and also denied that Syme's policy would in the long run be advantageous: 'What inducements would students have to attend the University when they could get the necessary information nearer home, and probably in some places at a cheaper rate?' Syme's plan 'would tend, instead of drawing students to Universities, to scatter them amongst the inferior and irresponsible schools'. When the town council in 1842 proposed to place extra-mural teachers on a position of virtual equality with the professors, the professors closed their ranks and argued that such recognition should be conditional and partial, not unconditional nor applicable to most of the curriculum. In 1845 however the Senatus recognised as qualifying for the MD degree extra-mural teaching at the London hospitals; but an application from Queen's College, Birmingham for similar recognition was rejected in 1846 on the ground that provincial schools of medicine were likely to be less efficient in instructing students than 'metropolitan establishments'. When in 1847 the town council made regulations which recognised courses of lectures, to be given by extra-mural teachers in Edinburgh itself, as qualifying for graduation, the Senatus took action in the law courts but lost their case.

By this time the indenture system, under which most eighteenth-century doctors and surgeons had been trained as apprentices to some person already in practice, had ceased altogether in Edinburgh and was on its way out in the other large towns of Britain. Since it was now generally agreed that to safeguard the public all medical and surgical practitioners should be trained both in theory and practice and their proficiency attested by an examining body, the Scottish corporations were eager to extend their system of licensing practitioners in the neighbourhood of Edinburgh and Glasgow to cover the whole of the British empire. The University of Edinburgh, whose MD degrees had for long been coveted as a proof of professional competence both in medicine and surgery, naturally resented the attempts of the medical and surgical corporations in the British Isles to gain control of the licensing of physicians and surgeons everywhere in the British empire at the very time when the decay of the indenture system afforded opportunities of attracting to itself greatly increased numbers of medical students.

Repeated attempts were made between 1834 and 1858 to reconcile the opposing interests of the medical and surgical incorporations, both in Scotland and elsewhere, with their extra-mural teachers of surgery and medicine, and of the universities, which provided medical education and degrees. Both sides had their parliamentary spokesmen and engaged in active lobbying. This, combined with pressure on government time, in a period notable for political and social reforms, brought about the postponement or defeat of several medical bills, notably Sir James Graham's which was introduced under Sir Robert Peel in the 1840s. Another attempt was made by Mr Headlam, MP for Newcastle upon Tyne, in 1855 and again in 1856, to which the Medical Faculty strongly objected. 'The main tendency of the bill', they believed, 'is to make all universities subordinate to the medical corporations; to discourage the superior education got at universities; to interpose so many mechanical and pecuniary obstructions in the way of intending practitioners, and so much difficulty in the shape of a lengthened curriculum, and of age, that the profession will be thinned out, the numerous poor districts of the country will be deprived of medical men altogether, and great encouragement will be given to unlicensed practitioners'.

This bill was defeated, partly by the vigorous opposition of the Edinburgh Faculty of Medicine; and in the following year the three interested Scottish universities, Marischal College in Aberdeen, Glasgow, and Edinburgh, agreed on a scheme for reforming medical education, not merely in order to establish uniformity amongst themselves, but to accommodate their uniform practice to that of the English and Irish universities. The key feature of this arrangement was to be the substitution of the degree of bachelor of medicine for that of doctor, which would henceforth be given only after further study to bachelors of medicine, except that a few doctorates of medicine might be given each year to qualified practitioners over the age of forty who had been in general practice for at least fifteen years. Unless they were already graduates in Arts of a British university, candidates must pass an examination in Arts and Philosophy before undergoing their first professional examination for the degree of bachelor of medicine. Arts graduates might present themselves after three years' professional study, others after four years, for the final degree examination. Bachelors of medicine would be entitled to practise equally surgery and medicine, and midwifery as a branch of medicine. Doctors of medicine only should rank as physicians. Finally, the Scottish universities claimed 'equal privileges and rights of practice for their graduates with those conceded to the licentiates, members, and fellows of the Incorporated Colleges'. The University of Edinburgh was entrusted with the delicate task of forming a common British university front against the excessive claims of the incorporations.

In the following year the passing of the Medical Act of 1858 provided a satisfactory solution of some of these long-standing difficulties. This Act set up the General Medical Council, partly elected by the universities and Royal Colleges, partly nominated by the Crown. This body kept a register of those qualified to practise medicine in any part of the British dominions, thus removing any chance of discrimination, for example in England against Edinburgh graduates or diplomates. It was also given the judicial function of removing from this register any practitioner guilty of crime or of professional misconduct.

THE FACULTY OF ARTS AND ITS CRITICS

Although the decline of the Arts Faculty was probably less conspicuous than that of Medicine in the early nineteenth century, it was also unmistakable. The common-sense school of philosophy had shot its bolt, Hallam and Macaulay had superseded Robertson and Hume, and the Chair of Rhetoric was held by men who, if remembered at all, are not usually regarded as great teachers. Dunbar, professor of Greek for forty-seven years and Pillans, his colleague in Humanity, (1820–63), were accomplished teachers and active University politicians, but did little to advance the boundaries of their subject. Byron's sneer at 'paltry Pillans', although probably less justified than many of the poet's criticisms, is still remembered. John Wilson was popular with his students, but much better known as a journalist under the pen name, Christopher North, than as a moral philosopher. *The Scotsman* argued that Wilson's published work proved his 'perverted taste and total incompetence . . . to fill the Chair of Moral Philosophy'; and the very appointment of Wilson, an Oxford alumnus, to one of the key appointments in the faculty shows how far the Scottish school of philosophy had decayed and indicates that it was not nepotism and inbreeding which caused the decline of the faculty. Soon Wilson was to be joined from the southern universities by Kelland in the Chair of Mathematics. Another Oxford man, who had, however, studied Medicine for a year at Edinburgh, was Sir William Hamilton. He held in succession the Chairs of Universal History and Logic, and spent much of his time quarrelling with his colleagues and attacking the town council.

The first thorough-going criticism of the Faculty of Arts in *Peter's Letters to his Kinsfolk*, published at Edinburgh in 1819, was the work of Walter Scott's son-in-law and biographer, J. G. Lockhart. Edinburgh students did not wear gowns nor live 'within the walls of colleges': they just went once or twice a day to listen to a lecture. They came up too young, with little Latin and, unless they had been pupils of the Edinburgh High School, no Greek. The professors of Classics were 'schoolmasters in the strictest sense of the word' and needed neither depth nor elegance of scholarship to perform their duties. Long before the students could possibly become competent

classical scholars, they were rushed into the study of Rhetoric. Failure
to soak themselves in the Greek philosophers and Roman historians
meant that they could never really appreciate 'the Philosophy of life,
the enjoyment arising from the Fine Arts, and the study of History'.
In another letter Lockhart attacked the over-emphasis on intellect and
the mechanical mode of observation which he regarded as characteristic of the Scottish metaphysicians.

Lockhart then referred to 'the slovenly and dirty mass' of students
'with its contaminating atmosphere' in the classrooms. Whereas in
England the father of a family seldom thought of sending his son to
college unless he could afford to give him an allowance of some £300
per annum, in Scotland, 'any young man who can afford to wear a
decent coat, and live in a garret upon porridge and herrings, may, if
he pleases, come to Edinburgh, and pass through his academical
career, just as creditably as is expected or required' on £30 or even
much less a year. The Edinburgh style of education made the Edinburgh student a keen doubter and debater, but offered him little
prospect of 'any great increase in worldly goods' or 'any very valuable
stronghold of peaceful meditation'. Indeed, at the end of the day, he
might find himself, if not a burden on his relations, at least filling a
post for which so expensive a preparation was unnecessary.

Lockhart's final conclusion was, however, much less adverse than
his criticisms, if valid, would have justified. English and Scottish
universities had diverse objects and were 'both excellent in their
different ways'. Indeed 'each system might borrow something with
advantage from the other' and 'in our great empire we have need of
many kinds of men; it is necessary that we should possess, within our
own bounds, the means of giving to each kind that sort of preparation
which may best fit them for the life to which they are destined'.

Much more violent than Lockhart were the critics who followed in
his wake, such as the author of *The Modern Athens,* published in 1825.
The 'Athenian university . . . has sunk to rise no more'. The present
professors were no longer men of talent and eminence. The students
'know not much and the little that they do know is very far from
being accurate; but they state their opinions with a frowardness, and
support even their ignorance and their errors with a pertinacity, at
which you are quite astonished. Perhaps it is this precocity in assertion

---

35. Professor John Wilson (Christopher North); painted by Thomas Duncan.

LOGIC

36. Professor Sir William Hamilton and his students as depicted by one of
them, later Professor Edward Forbes, in *The University Maga.*, 1837.

which renders the Athenians so querulous and dogmatical after they grow up'. Edinburgh University was 'still the same dark globe [like the moon] without light, save that which it has at second hand from another'.

Such assertions, unsupported as they were by evidence, need not detain us longer; but Lockhart's criticism deserves further consideration. Its outstanding features are lack of originality and flair for journalism. It was the time when Lockhart's work was published that gave force to his criticisms and attracted public attention to them. The winning of the long war against Napoleon relaxed tension; and the resulting economic and social distress produced amongst thinking men a feeling of pessimism. One aspect of this was a tendency to question the validity of the academic assumptions of the eighteenth century. The problem of the relationship between a liberal education and professional preparation, which had hardly troubled the eighteenth century, now became important. But there was in issue a still more basic question: what was a liberal education? While some academics wished to undo what the eighteenth century had achieved and compel all Arts students to attend the precise classes prescribed for them in the sixteenth and seventeenth centuries, attempts to bring this about were vigorously resisted, not only by sectional interests, but by reformers who genuinely believed in experiments designed to bring the out-of-date university system into harmony with the political and social conditions of nineteenth-century Britain.

One of the most thorough though manifestly biased of these critics of the early nineteenth-century system of instruction in the Arts Faculty at Edinburgh was the Reverend Michael Russel, an ex-schoolmaster, a convert to Episcopacy and, although the son of an Edinburgh citizen, a graduate of Glasgow University. He had published, six years before Lockhart's *Letters,* his *View of the System of Education at present pursued in the Schools and Universities of Scotland.* So far as classics were concerned, Russel's main theses were that pupils should be kept at school until they had thoroughly mastered the Latin language and acquired a tolerable acquaintance with Greek. No matter how able or assiduous, the professors of Classics could not hope to produce classical scholars under the existing system, although, of the Scottish universities, Edinburgh was 'unquestionably the best classical seminary'.

Russel's severest strictures were reserved for the Edinburgh method of teaching philosophy solely by the lecture system to large classes, without any attempt to make attendance compulsory, much less to examine regularly the students who did attend lectures. He admitted that an eminent and specialist professor 'will afford a clearer light, and more extensive information to the student, than the discourses of a young tutor employed in teaching several branches of learning;' but 'a very extensive and brilliant display of knowledge, so far from being useful to lads who have still to learn the rudiments of mental science, only dazzles and bewilders them.' At Edinburgh, the philosophical lectures were 'only fit for grown-up gentlemen' and therefore worse than useless to most of the professors' auditors. 'The plan of teaching Philosophy at Edinburgh' therefore appeared to Russel 'to be decidedly the worst with which I am acquainted . . . everything is done by the professors and the students do nothing'.

Edinburgh's claim to distinction and superiority rested solely on 'the communication of knowledge' and not at all on 'the exercise and improvement of youthful talent'. The professors of Logic, Moral Philosophy, and Natural Philosophy delivered lectures five days a week, but made little if any further attempt to teach their students. Russel then proceeded to criticise Edinburgh's neglect of mathematics and particularly of geometry. With the changing character of Natural Philosophy mathematical knowledge had become a better introduction to it than formal logic; yet Edinburgh students could 'listen to the most profound and intricate demonstrations in physical science without having read the Elements of Euclid'.

Edinburgh's final sin of omission was the absence of 'daily and yearly examinations'. Amongst her students 'the glow of emulation and the ardour of competition are never felt. There reigns an uninterrupted stagnation of animal spirits, an eternal sinecure within her walls; and those young men only who are smitten with the love of science, and pursue her for her own sake, can be supposed to study at all'. Worse still, in spite of the 'wretched system of academical instruction . . . several hundred young men come up annually to Edinburgh, without anyone to guide their studies, or keep alive their industry; and who, as they are, generally speaking, unknown to their teacher even by name, can enjoy nothing of that encouragement and friendly admonition, which are so necessary amid a thousand temptations to idleness and vice'. Russel found it hard to understand why such an inferior system of education attracted to Edinburgh far more Arts students than to the rival and educationally much superior institutions, especially when he calculated that 'a complete course at

College' cost £28 7s. in fees at Edinburgh, £16 10s. at St Andrews or Glasgow, and only £11 11s. at Aberdeen.

Although it may be admitted that some of his criticisms are shrewd, Russel must be regarded as a reactionary. He had no idea of broadening an out-of-date curriculum, and no appreciation of the importance of student societies. His ideal was a return to the sixteenth century at the expense of nearly all that had been gained in the eighteenth. He even quoted with manifest satisfaction the precedent of Robert Rollock's regular use of corporal punishment. What gave weight to his criticisms was that amongst the old ideas and practices which he wished to resurrect was the tutorial system both of instruction and supervision of students, which had, in its ancient form, been already outgrown at Edinburgh. Here at least he enjoyed powerful backing from English critics and from the Anglophile reformers of the Scottish universities.

THE COMPLETION OF THE OLD COLLEGE BUILDING

Another drawback to the advancement of the University, in the first half of the nineteenth century, which affected equally the Faculties of Arts and Medicine, was the state of its accommodation. The first government grant of £5,000, given in 1801, was intended merely to prevent further deterioration of the unfinished new building. The fall of Pitt's ministry in the same year and the reopening of the war with France threw the Trustees for College buildings back upon their own almost invisible resources. In 1805 they were considering the prospect of raising money by a public lottery. Merely to finish building the north and east fronts would cost £32,973, while huge sums would be needed to fit out the interior. Sir John Carr, a well-informed visitor to Edinburgh in 1807, wrote that Adam's 'august but unfinished pile excites sentiments both of admiration and regret'. To complete the College building, which 'would be infinitely too vast for its objects', would cost at least £120,000. Even if completed, the building would lose much of its dignity by not receding to a proper distance from the street.*

Delay and inflation had rendered Adam's grandiose plans impracticable. The professors who had failed to get accommodation in the new buildings now compiled a list of what they considered necessary

---

* Carr, *Caledonian Sketches*, pp. 90–1.

and this was sent by the Senatus to the town council in 1808. Between 1809 and 1811 Robert Reid was employed by the town council to prepare drawings and estimates of the cost of completing the University on this reduced plan. It may have been Reid who first suggested turning the two Adam quadrangles into one, although another architect, Morrison, had publicly exhibited in 1810 'a design for altering the plan of the College, by throwing it into one Court, without altering any thing that is already executed'. At the same time the town council secured the support of the Convention of Royal Burghs for their contention that completion of the buildings was an object of national importance to Scotland. They calculated that only eleven classrooms in the old and new parts of the College buildings were available for twenty-four professors, some of whom taught for two or three hours a day. The Divinity classroom, shared also by the professor of Hebrew, was so badly lighted that candles had to be used all day. And the number of students had increased in the twenty years since the laying of the foundation stone from about 1,000 to nearly 2,000.

Robert Dundas, MP for Edinburghshire, had, in 1813, hoped to obtain £5,000 from the first lord of the Treasury, Lord Liverpool, by urging upon him the precedent of Pitt's grant in 1801; but it was not until the end of the war, and after the presentation of a petition to Parliament, that news arrived that a government grant of £10,000 a year would be made to complete and furnish the buildings, under the control of the 'College Commission'. By a happy coincidence successive town council votes on the same day thanked the Lord Provost for sending them, by express, news of the glorious battle of Waterloo and for helping to obtain a grant of £10,000 for the College 'with every prospect of the like sum being annually granted for seven years'. At the end of the war the existing buildings of the College, according to Necker de Saussure, were 'le plus bizarre mélange d'ancien et de nouveau, de magnificence et de pauvreté.'

By this time each professor had stated what he required in the way of accommodation for his classes and the Commission decided on 12 September 1816 to exclude from the building-scheme provision for professors' houses and the proposed cross-buildings. This would allow them to find the required accommodation in a single large quadrangle and thus save expense. Along with houses for the principal and librarian, classrooms were to be provided for Divinity, Theology, and Law on the east side; for Medicine, including Chemistry,

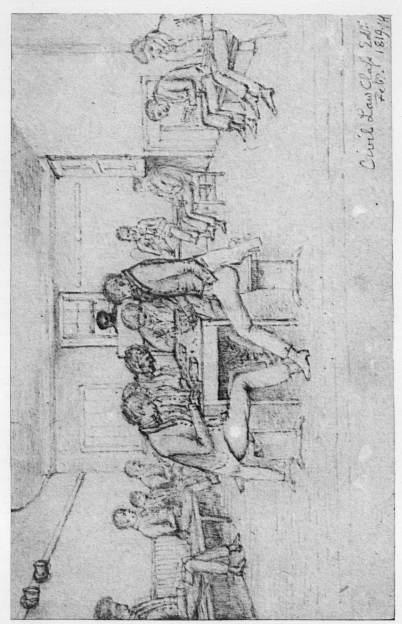

37. The Civil Law classroom; pencil sketch by James Hall, 1819.

Anatomy, and the practice of Medicine on the north; and for Literature and Philosophy, along with the Library and the Natural History
Museum, on the south. The west side was to contain the great hall
for public assemblies which could also be used as a College chapel.

Several well-known architects submitted plans on these lines to the
Commission. They included William Adam (brother of Robert) and
Morrison, who had assisted Robert Adam for many years; but the
Commissioners, largely influenced by the advice of the Senatus,
preferred the plans of a young and unknown competitor, W. H.
Playfair, who had convinced the Senatus that he could provide the
accommodation they desired with the least possible alteration of
Adam's design and at less cost than most of the other competitors.
The Commissioners gave priority to the provision of classrooms and
the Divinity hall was the first to be finished (1817). By 1819 the
actual building of the 'spacious and splendid apartments' needed for
the Natural History Museum on the west side of the quadrangle had
been completed but the interior fitting up of this block presented
problems. Moreover a pressure group, consisting of the professors of
Natural Philosophy, Mathematics, Greek, Humanity, and Logic,
claimed in 1820 to be very ill accommodated and demanded preferential treatment. Nevertheless the lower room of the Museum could
be used for the medical graduation on 1 August 1820 and 'formed a
magnificent Doric hall.'

Two new rooms were appropriated for the use of the Senatus in
1822; but the town council refused to provide furnishings for them.
Nevertheless, the Senate met for the first time on 26 August 1822 in
the new hall and resolved solemnly that it should be called the Senate
Hall. The Museum was still unfinished, partly owing to the large
number of exhibits which were being received and which had to be
temporarily stored in odd corners of the buildings. Urgent memorials
and petitions in 1822–3 were successful in securing continuance of
the annual government grant of £10,000. The Senatus by this time
had raided Library funds for the money, amounting to £22 17s.,
needed to equip the Senate rooms. Hearth rugs for each room and a
mirror for the mantelpiece of the principal room were procured along
with newspapers, *Reviews*, and books of general interest. The best
pictures were to be removed from the Library, cleaned, and used to
adorn the walls. A register of the weather was to be regularly kept by
the professor of Mathematics and a thermometer and books were
provided for this purpose.

38. The Museum of Natural History (now the New Reading Room);
an engraving by W. H. Lizars. Note the puma, which was supposed
to have the run of the museum.

By 1823 the Natural History Museum had also been completely
fitted up and the Commissioners turned their main attention to the
Library. In 1819 there had been doubts, removed however by an
architect's report from Playfair, whether it would be safe to hold the
medical graduation in the old Library.* Years before, this building
had lost its north end, and the 30,000 volumes which were still in the
upper rooms of this block in 1823, were exposed to the weather. The
part still standing was in danger of suddenly tumbling down and had
to be supported by wooden beams resting against the new buildings
'without which it could not stand a single day'. W. H. Lizars was
employed to make four engravings, which would bring out the incon-
gruity of the old and new buildings and convince the Treasury Lords
that the ruinous old buildings exposed 'the lives of the professors and
students to perpetual and imminent hazard'. These engravings were
attached to a memorial from Senatus to the Lords of the Treasury

* This refers to the earlier of the two Library buildings constructed in the
first half of the seventeenth century, viz., that commenced in 1616.

39. The 1617 Building from the south-east; one of four engravings by Lizars and Basire which were commissioned in 1823 as propaganda to ensure further parliamentary grants towards the cost of the new buildings.

and were copied by James Basire for reproduction in the relevant volume of parliamentary papers. The Senatus added other arguments, mainly that one-third of Edinburgh Chairs were filled on the nomination of the Crown, and that the number of students had continued to increase until it had reached, in 1823, an all-time record of 2,400.

These arguments secured continuation of the grant of £10,000 for another four years and enabled Playfair to design the great hall of the Library and to complete the quadrangle. In the summer of 1827 the books were being transferred to the new apartments, although most of them had had to be moved twice, first to certain classrooms, then, once the cases had been removed from the old Library and fitted up in a temporary way in the graduation hall, the books were replaced on their former shelves. Until 'the great room' was finished, no person

40. The east front of the Old College; drawn by Shepherd and engraved by
Lizars, 1829.

was to be allowed access to the interior of the Library; but 'a reading
room for students' was 'nearly ready' in November 1827, and special
temporary arrangements would be made for the professors. The old
Library building was then demolished and some of the inscriptions
which had adorned the walls of the Old College buildings in Hebrew,
Greek, and Latin were built into the wall of the vestibule leading to
the present Court Room. No provision was in the end made either
for a College chapel or a graduation hall. Once the Natural History
Museum was fitted up in the western hall this could no longer be used
for graduation ceremonies; and for many years the large Chemistry
classroom served for the annual medical graduations on 1 August.

Some internal alterations were made about this time in the Adam
buildings, especially at the north-west corner of the quadrangle. The
Adam Anatomy theatre, 60 feet in height, was divided horizontally
at first-floor level and the middle lights of the great three-light windows
to the north and west, which had been blocked up, were reopened.
The ground floor was then fitted up as an anatomical museum at an
estimated cost of £1,500, while the lecture theatre above was used for
lectures and demonstrations until the anatomists removed with their

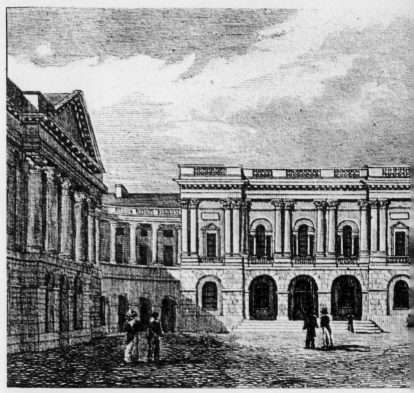

41. An engraving from Stark's *Picture of Edinburgh*, 1829, showing the
quadrangle before the building of the raised walk along the south,
west, and north sides.

medical colleagues to Teviot Place.* The last important structural
work in connection with the present Old College was the completion
of the 'College Court' by the erection of the raised walk on three
sides, with 'angular' flights of steps giving access to the classrooms
from the level floor of the quadrangle. Flights of steps from the
principal entrances to the college north and south of the carriage
entrance also gave pedestrians access to the raised walk. The total
cost of this scheme amounted to £2,400 and the work was carried out
during the session 1832–3.

---

* See D. B. Horn, 'The Anatomy Classrooms in the present Old College,
1725–1880' in *Univ. of Edin. Journal* (Spring 1965), pp. 65–71.

Partly to reduce the danger of fire, partly to improve the lighting of the Museum, tumbledown property to the west of the College was purchased and demolished and the Commissioners hoped also to buy and demolish property on the other side of North College (now Chambers) Street, move the line of this street to the north and plant the intervening space with ornamental trees. In the outcome, however, these admirable proposals for providing the new building with a spacious and dignified setting came to naught; and in the 1860s the last open space around the College and immediately to the west of the Natural History Museum, was occupied by part of the building now known as the Royal Scottish Museum.

The government grant of £10,000 was regularly paid up to 1826 inclusive, when the Tory government wearied apparently of well-doing; and it was not until the Whigs came into office that the remaining sum of £6,000 required to meet the estimated cost was paid in 1832. This final government contribution seems to have been due in part to the good offices of Lord Chancellor Brougham. After the fall of the Whigs in 1834 the Commissioners for College Buildings asked in 1835 for a statement of what was still defective in the accommodation provided for the University, but no action seems to have resulted. The new Prime Minister, Sir Robert Peel, and his colleagues showed no sympathy; and indeed by this time any money which could be extracted from a parsimonious government could be better applied, in the opinion of most of the professors, to other purposes than buildings.

Playfair had listed in January 1832 various respects in which the new buildings were defective – the absence of any provision for the needs of the newly created Chairs of Surgery and Pathology, the confusion and congestion in the University museums, the inadequacy of the Chemical laboratory and its equipment, the temporary shelving in the Theological Library, etc. In later life, when engaged in a wrangle with the Trustees over the size of Donaldson's hospital, he quoted the University and the Register House as outstanding examples of Edinburgh buildings which had proved too small adequately to meet the purposes for which they had been built. Sir William Hamilton particularly deplored in 1839 the want of a College chapel and of a hall for various academical ceremonies, including graduation.

Expenditure on this scale was beyond the resources of the town council; but, probably influenced by the snowball riots of 1838, they accepted in 1839 an estimate from 'the Shotts Iron Company – being the lowest – to furnish and erect three gates on the principal front of the College, agreeably to Mr Playfair's drawings and specifications for £166'. The gates were erected in 1840. Professor Baldwin Brown not long after his appointment to the Chair of Fine Art, found himself immured in the College late at night. Trying to break out by climbing one of the gates, he was promptly arrested by a police constable who was convinced the professor was a criminal trying to break into the College. Adorned by legend, the gates still look out on the South Bridge.

When in 1854 the government proposed to build a new museum on the Trades Maiden Hospital site to the west of the University, the Senate tried unsuccessfully to link this scheme with the erection of a common hall which would serve the purpose of a Music classroom

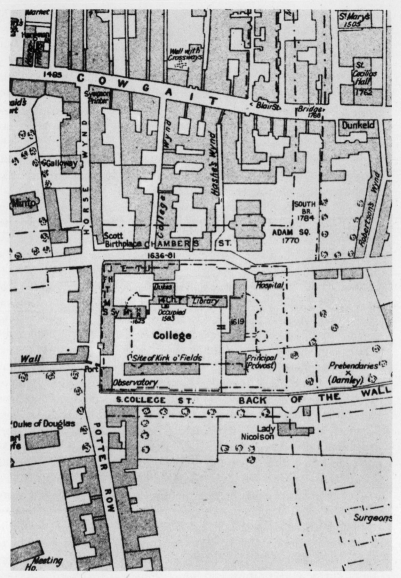

42. A reconstruction, by Henry F. Kerr, of the University and its environs, *c.* 1750, superimposed on the Ordnance Survey map of 1851, which is shown by dotted lines; from *The Book of the Old Edinburgh Club*, 1922.

as well and towards which the Senate would contribute £5,000 out of the Reid Fund.

THE QUARREL BETWEEN TOWN COUNCIL AND SENATUS

Yet another drawback to the progress of the University in this period was the protracted quarrel between the town council and the Senate, which bulks so largely in the contemporary sources for the history of the University. This need not detain us long. The issues directly raised are dead as mutton; what matters now are the indirect consequences of the quarrel. Perhaps the earliest sign of divergence may be detected in the different attitudes adopted to the creation, soon after 1800, of new Regius Medical and Surgical Chairs. The town council adopted its now customary line of theoretical protest and practical acceptance, but some of the professors concerned resented what they regarded as the supineness of the council in defending the legal rights and financial profits of the older Medical Chairs. Other professors, by 1808, felt that the council was not doing all it could do to remove 'the inconveniences experienced by the University from the unfinished state of the new buildings.' When in the same year the Senate, on its own authority, without any consultation with the town council, raised the fees to be charged for graduation, the medical students protested to the council, which at once claimed that any alteration of fees, if not done directly by the council, certainly required their previous consent. The council clearly regarded what had been done as the thin end of the wedge and sent the Senate voluminous extracts from their records 'relative to the superintendence and direction claimed by the magistrates in the affairs of the College.' In 1809 also they drew up revised regulations for the Library which caused considerable debate in the Senate.

The Senate now began to question the administration by the town council of the benefactions received for the benefit of the College. Although what may perhaps be described as the original cause of the quarrel was removed in 1812 when the town raised fees for tuition to the level previously advocated by the Senate and now accepted by them, the Senate continued to pester the council with unimportant queries about their financial administration. When Monro *secundus* died the College bailie demanded the keys of the Anatomy museum, since it had been part of the bargain made by Monro with the town council when the new Anatomy theatre had been built, that his anatomical specimens should become the property of the town council on his death. The keys were reluctantly handed over and it was not until some years later, in 1823, that the Senate discovered that by a later will Monro had bequeathed his collection not to the town council but to the University. While all this was going on, a Senate committee had been solemnly considering the relations between the patrons and the Senatus. It searched for evidence among Dalzel's manuscripts and tried, vainly of course, to recover from the patrons 'the early College minutes supposed to be in possession of the patrons'.

What finally brought matters to a head was the claim of the professor of Midwifery to be a member of the Faculty of Medicine and as such entitled to examine candidates for graduation and to collect a share of the fees payable by the candidates. When Hamilton's claim met with the reception that he must have expected from his colleagues, he appealed to the town council, which forwarded it to the Senate. On a report from the Medical Faculty which was favourable to the introduction of Midwifery as a compulsory subject for the MD degree as part of a 'very extensive and important system of alterations', but which also expressed the hope that the Senatus would not acknowledge any 'right of authoritative interference by the patrons in such matters', the Senatus resolved that 'the sole right to originate and carry into execution every regulation respecting the course of study to be followed for candidates for medical degrees' was among the 'various powers, privileges, and immunities which belong to the University itself exclusively, and which arise from the essential and indefeasable nature and character of an University, from the written law of the land, and from the effect of immemorial and unchallenged usage'.

The town council retorted by giving Hamilton a new commission expressly naming him a member of the Faculty of Medicine; and on 10 November 1825 the Lord Provost, magistrates, and council formally 'visited' the University in order to give their own regulation requiring attendance by medical students on the Midwifery and the Diseases of Women and Children class 'the character of a law of the College'. Headed by their principal, sixteen professors claimed in reply that the Senatus alone had the privilege and power of making regulations binding upon their students. The issue was now joined before the Court of Session, which decided in 1829 in favour of the town council. No other decision was possible for a court of law, as the Senatus found when they again engaged in legal proceedings against the town council, and carried their case on appeal to the House of Lords in the 1840s.

Even before the date of the formal visitation, the Senatus was engaged on an extra-judicial appeal to George IV 'as the paramount protector and patron of the University' to appoint commissioners to investigate the matters in dispute between themselves and the town council. It was this petition to the Crown which brought about the appointment of a royal commission to visit the Scottish universities in 1826, much to the annoyance of some members of the other universities, who were very comfortable as they were and resented the east wind of enquiry and the prospect of change.

SOCIAL LIFE, DISCIPLINE, AND STUDENT RECREATIONS

Such evidence as has survived about social contacts between Edinburgh professors in the eighteenth century has been reviewed in the preceding chapter. In 1792 a 'social annual convention' was formed to try to bring them together at least once a year. This came to be called the symposium and flourished for many years. In 1824 the staple dishes served at the annual dinner were roast beef and plum pudding 'and the mirth [was] abundantly noisy'. In 1826 the club 'did not separate till a late hour, having partaken of oysters and toddy, after tea and coffee'. In 1848 after dinner they adjourned to the Calton Hill Observatory where the professor of Astronomy 'enlightened his colleagues by an exhibition of the starry heavens through his powerful telescope'. The menus were often drawn up in Latin and French and at least once in Greek. Aytoun on one occasion recited 'The Massacre of the Macpherson'; various professors gave 'musical performances' including a song on the varied uses of glass by Professor Bennett, which proved so popular with his colleagues that it was repeated at later meetings. At least once (in 1873) the Regius Keeper of the Botanic Garden supplied home-grown bananas as an addition to the menu.

There is also much more evidence about student life in the first half of the nineteenth century than in any earlier period; and the evidence is much more direct and explicit. Instead of arguing from seventeenth-century Latin rules, consisting mainly of prohibitions, and wondering how far they were relevant to eighteenth-century conditions, we can now read many letters and other contemporary evidence written by the students themselves. Nevertheless, as late as

43. The menu and bill of fare for the annual dinner of the Professors' Club, 1817.

1841 an attempt was to be made to codify the rules to which students were subject.

Several short-lived student magazines appeared in this period, inevitably intent upon criticising the existing state of the University, and offering suggestions for its improvement in various ways, often contradictory to each other. The best was *The University Maga* (1835, 1837–8), notable for its drawings by Edward Forbes, later to become professor of Natural History at Edinburgh. Most were ephemeral and disappeared without trace after one or two issues as did the *University Boreas* of 1846. Occasionally one would survive for a whole session; and even, like *The Cheilead or University Coterie* of 1826–7 achieve the dignity of being reprinted at the end of the year.

The Cheilead was not the first student magazine, but it was typical of student journalism to the present day in its choice of topics and its mingled censure and defence of the student body. One contributor complained 'there is not such a disjointed body of alumni in the whole world' as at Edinburgh. 'A proper place' should be provided and students recommended, but not forced, to live there under the supervision of honest and moral persons. This would avoid much of the immorality charged against students, but often due rather to their landladies, and would give Edinburgh undergraduates a better chance of mixing, which would be useful to them in later life.

Other contributors to *The Cheilead* commented upon the opening of the Anatomical museum, denounced avaricious professors who prescribed their own expensive text-books for their classes, suggested coyly that in opening a class to instruct ladies in Natural Philosophy Professor Leslie was looking for a wife, or deplored the change in student recreations from out-of-door games, such as football and archery, to billiards. One writer described the town council as 'a set of ignorant and mercenary boobies', and claimed for the student body the patronage of all university Chairs. A meeting of students was actually held in the Natural Philosophy classroom a few years later (1833) and an attempt made to influence the election of a new professor of this subject. But the *pièce de resistance* in this slim volume was the prototype of dozens of articles purporting to describe the undergraduate career of a typical Edinburgh student:

An indulgence in the *otium vitae,* without dignity or propriety,
are the distinguishing characteristics of the Edinburgh students.
They no sooner rise than they concert plans for killing the day;
the Agency office – the peep at the College – the slow lounge from

street to street – the Tennis Court – jellies, soups and the bet at
whist – the mace, the cue, the ride, the newest novel – each in
turn engages the mind. The day killed . . . they begin to think of
spending the night. This includes the dinner – 'where shall we
dine?' . . . 'Tis ten to one the watch-house, or some worse place,
vomits them forth in the morning, pale, nervous and debili-
tated. . . . The *last year* – the midnight paper – the pale sickly cast –
uneasiness of mind – anxiety – and probably pecuniary difficulties,
now in their turn take the lead. Then health, already declining,
receives the finishing stroke. They are ashamed – they study, and
study hard, and pass – showing what may be done by resolution
and perseverance. They depart from Edinburgh and, for the most
part without one sigh, one longing, lingering look. . . . Whose
fault is this? [no pastime is provided for them except the theatre
and when they tire of this they go to the billiard room and the
tavern]. Cannot some society [for amusement] be formed or club
instituted among the students?

There is however better evidence than this of the importance of
taverns in student life. In 1851 Principal Lee brought to the notice
of the Senatus 'repeated cases of intoxication on the part of certain
medical students'. Two other medical students who had been drunk
and disorderly spent the Christmas holidays of 1851–2 in jail. In 1853
the Senatus appointed a committee to look into the matter of 'the
taverns which are multiplying in the neighbourhood of the College',
and a group of students started a Total Abstinence Society whose
operations soon 'assumed very extensive proportions'.

This particular problem was connected with the more general
question of maintaining discipline. In most cases student misbehaviour
could be treated as a domestic concern, even when it took the
form of persistent bullying, striking another student in the course
of an examination, discharging pistols in the Anatomy classroom, or
challenging a fellow-student to a duel. Such cases were carefully
enquired into and, as a rule, an appropriate penalty promptly inflicted
by the Senatus, ranging from reprimand to expulsion. Only one case
of this kind gave the Senatus much trouble. When the professor of
Divinity in 1812 refused to allow one of his students, John Ross, to
offer his remarks on discourses delivered by other students in the
Divinity hall, Ross publicly accused his professor of 'tyranny, injustice,
and oppression' and was promptly expelled by the Senatus. Ross
retaliated by publishing a pamphlet on *The Present State of the Edinburgh*

Divinity Hall and argued his case before the General Assembly. Finally, on receiving an apology from the offender, the Senatus recalled the sentence of expulsion in 1815. More than once the Senatus announced its determination to suppress stamping and hissing in University classes and a formal enquiry by the Senatus into disturbances of this kind in the third Monro's class was averted by the professor's resignation.

In 1812 the Senatus believed that the basic cause of these disorders was the indolence and incompetence of the two janitors, whose offices had for long been treated as sinecures. Two new janitors were appointed and their duties carefully defined; but no improvement resulted. No sooner were the new buildings completed than there were complaints that students were cutting the woodwork and defacing the walls of classrooms. There was a lack of liaison between the janitors and the private servants of the professors, some of whom were no older than the students, and lacked the ability, and sometimes the inclination, to back up the professor's or janitor's attempt to maintain order. Even formal University occasions, such as the reading of prize essays or the early Reid Concerts, sometimes degenerated into riots. It was not until late in the nineteenth century that the tradition of employing veteran soldiers as servitors became firmly established.

A new list of duties of the janitor and porter was drawn up in 1832–3 and again in 1840. By this time the offices of secretary of the University, responsible to the town council, and secretary to Senatus, a post held by a professor, had been separated; and the Senatus no longer felt the same responsibility for the physical control of turbulent students within the University, since the janitor now reported through the secretary of the University direct to the town council. Nevertheless, in 1854, the Senatus showed their dissatisfaction with the existing arrangement by appointing a committee to consider, by the institution of proctors or otherwise, the keeping of order among students. The Committee's solution, the appointment of a Committee of Discipline consisting of four professors, one from each faculty, was still-born. Apart from physical violence, few cases of breach of academic rules were brought to the notice of the Senatus. Very rarely, students were charged with dishonest practices in connection with examinations and in one or two cases they were expelled.

---

44. Student high-jinks in Professor John Playfair's class; from a student notebook of 1811, possibly that of Lord John Russell. Under Playfair the teaching of Natural Philosophy was becoming less Aristotelian and more experimental.

Battle of the Quadrangle

45. The Snowball Riots of 1838 as seen by Edward Forbes; from *The University Maga*, 1838.

More serious was the problem of student disorder when it involved third parties. The centuries-old bickering between the younger students and the High School boys continued into the nineteenth century and led to the notorious snowball riots of the 1830s and 1840s. In view of the University's peculiar relationship to the town council there could be at Edinburgh no town and gown conflict of laws. Even when, in 1818, one student assaulted another on the steps going up to the Anatomy classroom, the Senate decided to await the outcome of his trial in the police court. *A fortiori* when students threw snowballs at passers-by and became involved in a fracas with the police, they were tried on a charge of 'mobbing, rioting, and assault' before the Sheriff-Substitute. The most that the Senate could do was to appoint a committee to attend the trial and try to make sure 'that the truth be properly expiscated in regard to the relative portion of blame' attributable to students, mob, and police. This was in 1838, although less serious disturbances of the same kind had occurred in 1831 and were to recur in the forties and fifties. The 1838 riots left behind them an extensive, if not valuable, collection of student verses, most of them parodies of Byron, Campbell, and Scott.

While Louis Philippe's ministers were alleged to suspect that the riot of 1838 was 'part of a general revolutionary insurrection among the university students of Europe', the Senatus welcomed student expressions of opinion that the riots were partly due to dissatisfaction with the existing government of the University by the town council. The Senatus were, however, anxious to prevent any recurrence of trouble and discussed methods of preventing it with the town council from time to time. Yet when a group of students proposed to introduce the wearing of gowns in 1843 a committee of Senatus reported that this would be 'inexpedient and unproductive of any of the advantages which in earlier times were expected to result from it'. The students who had expressed their opinions were equally divided for and against, while 'a still greater number appear to have taken no interest in the matter'.

This conclusion is probably equally applicable to another old problem of student life—attendance at Lady Yester's Church for Sunday services. In 1821, as part of a general scheme of reforms, each faculty was instructed to send a deputation to attend church at the head of their students; but there is no reason to think that this was more effective than previous arrangements. When in 1825 Lady Yester's Church was under repair, Professor Hope's classroom was used for public worship. Soon the students returned to Lady Yester's and, in the opinion of a Senatus committee headed by Thomas Chalmers, behaved themselves with 'perfect decorum and propriety', although the gallery was completely filled, with students standing at the back, and no professors present. The committee was so ignorant of past history that it described as a novelty its own recommendation that one or two professors should attend in rotation each Sunday. With the Disruption there was for some time the possibility that adherents of the established church would continue to worship in Lady Yester's while the free churchmen, under the patronage of the town council, would be allotted the Chemistry classroom as a dissenting chapel.

The use of rooms in the College for non-academic purposes, under authority of the town council, remained a red rag to the Senatus until the passing of the 1858 Act. They were also repeatedly concerned about the holding of meetings in College rooms by student societies. In 1795 the danger of fire so alarmed the Senatus that they ordered all meetings of student societies to be transferred from the new to the old buildings. In 1821 a committee of Senatus listed among the fire risks the holding of meetings of student societies which often broke up so late 'that it is to be feared that due attention may not be given to guard against accidents'. On the completion of the new buildings student societies were at first excluded from meeting in them. Playfair expressed alarm in 1832 that the continued exclusion of student societies would result in loss of Parliamentary grant and consequently make it impossible to complete the building. Some of the societies however joined together to form the 'Associated Societies' and, with the help of Lord Cockburn, they were able to secure their return to University premises in 1833 on condition that effectual precautions were taken against 'danger or impropriety'. The town council believed that 'the nightly convocations of male philosophers led to the attendance of scientific females within the walls of the quadrangle' and thus made it easy for 'disrespectable prowlers' to 'make their nocturnal haunts within the academic premises'.

In spite of these difficulties, student societies continued to flourish and many new ones were founded. All were primarily and many of them exclusively debating societies and there were constant complaints about the lack of a student social centre. On the other hand, the most prominent Edinburgh alumni of this period, writing in mature life about their student days, are virtually unanimous in testifying to the enjoyment which they derived from membership of debating societies and to the advantages which membership of such societies afforded them in later life.

There would appear to be little change in student recreations in this period from those which were popular in the later eighteenth century. No doubt many students would visit Weir's Museum of Natural History which occupied premises in the South Bridge about 1800. A little later a menagerie and circus with a royal Bengal tiger occupied a site in front of the College and seems to have been well patronised. In 1815 by special permission of the Senatus, Mr Sadler was authorised to use the College quadrangle 'for ascending in his balloon'. There is one reference to the playing of shinty within the college yard in 1810, punished by a fine. Snowballing, throwing stones, playing billiards, and any form of gambling or duelling continued to be repressed, and, when detected, punished by the authorities. Since there was no provision for meals in the College, it was difficult to punish students who claimed that they visited taverns not to drink but to obtain a midday meal. In 1850 the Senatus, forgetting that a bawdy classical play had been performed within the College by some of its students and other youngsters in 1681, expressed its disapproval of 'University theatricals'.

In vacations the improvement in means of communication both in Lowlands and Highlands made it easier for students to explore Scotland. Pedestrian tours became fashionable when some of the professors gave a lead and showed how a pleasurable excursion could be combined with pursuit of academic study of the natural sciences. Natural philosophers, botanists, and geologists explored the Highlands and climbed the less accessible hills which had been neglected by their eighteenth-century precursors. These expeditions sometimes led to conflict with landlords, sporting tenants, and their gamekeepers, such as the celebrated battle of Glen Tilt of 1847 in which the Duke of Atholl sought to bar the way to Professor J. H. Balfour and some of his students. When the early history of Scottish mountaineering, as distinct from rock climbing, comes to be written, it will be found that professors and students played a leading part. For this some credit must be given to the Arts and Divinity long vacation, lasting from mid-April to early November.

Occasional voices were raised against this tradition: classical professors complained that their students after a session's study of Greek or Latin came back to the University at the beginning of the second

year knowing less of the language than they had done at the beginning of the first. But the long vacation was as attractive to the professors as it was essential to the students, many of whom earned during
the summer the money needed to maintain them at the University in
the following session. Almost the only attempt to end the traditional
system was made by John Farquhar of Fonthill Abbey who, knowing
from his own experience the evil results of the long vacation, left
money in his will to induce Scottish professors to lecture throughout
the summer by offering them a cash bonus. Attempts were also vainly
made by the Medical professors to end or curtail the short Christmas
vacation, but these were defeated by the opposition of the medical
students and the refusal of the other professors to back up their
medical colleagues.

CONTACTS WITH OTHER UNIVERSITIES, THE CHURCH, AND THE STATE

Contacts between Edinburgh and the other Scottish universities were
occasional and unimportant. From time to time, in accordance with
seventeenth- and eighteenth-century precedents, university conferences were held in Edinburgh, usually at the time of meeting of
the General Assembly. Such were the 1803–4 Conferences on the
Arts degree, presided over by Principal Baird; the 1819 Conference,
when the other universities adopted as their own an Edinburgh
memorial on the Copyright Acts, and also discussed the salaries of
the Theological professors; and the 1822 Conference (during George
IV's visit) concerned partly with the attempts by Marischal College
to secure exemption from the Militia Act for students of Scottish universities. Subsequent conferences were held on subjects of common
interest: for example the MA degree and the possibility of securing
complete uniformity of courses, subjects, and standards at the different
universities; the representation of the Scottish universities in Parliament; and the effects of various government proposals and taxes upon
the Medical Faculties, especially in the 1850s when rival bills for
regulating the medical profession were under parliamentary consideration. So far as I am aware, all these conferences took place in Edinburgh at times convenient to representatives of the other universities.
The practice of holding such conferences in the university which
seeks a conference is of recent growth.

The mid-nineteenth century is the period when the University

46. John Bristed and his companion on the visit to the Highlands described in his *Pedestrian Tour* (1803). Bristed is wearing the 'furry cap' which is sometimes referred to by later tourists.

severs most of its ancient links with the church and when it comes to be more and more closely linked with the state. This was a general tendency of the age, but is particularly marked at Edinburgh owing to the way in which the new buildings were directly financed by the government. Down to 1792 almost the only contact with the state had been the presentation of formal addresses to the Sovereign expressing the devotion of the University to the house of Hanover and the principles of Whiggery. Towards the end of the century and under the impulse of the French wars, Whiggery died a natural death and for a time diehard Toryism dominated the University. Successive attempts on the lives of the Sovereigns invariably produced a loyal address from the principal and professors deploring sedition, promising to bring up their students as devoted subjects, and insinuating that early indoctrination in the principles of Christianity was the best cure for sedition. In 1819 for example the Senatus attributed the all too prevalent 'disloyalty and insubordination' to 'unprincipled and artful demagogues' and the 'wide and assiduous circulation of impious publications and . . . insidious harangues of the public meetings of the people as full of infidelity as of sedition'.

On George IV's accession 'one of the professors' suggested that the address to the new Sovereign should not be entrusted for presentation to the MP for the city of Edinburgh but should be presented by a deputation of the Senatus. This may well have been a by-product of the increasing tension between town council and University. So gracious was the reception accorded to the deputation that this new method at once became a precedent. George IV told the principal that he thought it 'right and of importance that in times like the present the teachers of a great seminary should show to the public that their own principles are sound and constitutional'. The royal Dukes of Clarence and Sussex also 'professed their high sense of [the value of the University of Edinburgh] to the Empire'. Principal Baird also had interviews with the Prime Minister, Foreign Secretary, and Chancellor of the Exchequer. He returned home with promises of help in procuring specimens for the Natural History museum and avoiding damage to them in transit, as well as an agreement for the despatch of corpses to Edinburgh for dissection 'in any number and at any period of the year', and not only 'through a most respectable channel' but 'at the usual rate of cost'.

When two years later George IV paid his celebrated visit to Edinburgh, the professors took tickets at a cost of half a guinea each for places on a special platform to see the royal procession pass from Holyrood to the Castle. Any doubts about the stability of the platform were resolved by a favourable report from the University architect, Playfair, and the Senatus duly appeared 'robed in their gowns and with full-dress hats'. Practically the whole body of professors then trooped down to Holyrood to present their loyal address.

When George IV died, a deputation of the Senatus was again despatched to London with an address and reported that, in conferring with the ministers, 'a disposition was shown to favour the interests of the University especially by countenancing an additional grant for furnishing the buildings' which was paid soon after, and also a promise to have regard to the interests of the University in the projected new Anatomical Bill. Although the same procedure was followed on the accession of Queen Victoria, her ministers seem to have been less forthcoming than their predecessors.

By this time the loyal addresses were ceasing to be political manifestos. Principal Lee, for example, who drafted the address of 1840, prayed that her Majesty's reign 'may ever be distinguished by the advancement of learning and science, by the prevalence of enlightened piety and pure morals, and by the permanent establishment of social order and universal peace.' By this time also the other Scottish universities were following Edinburgh's example. When addresses were presented to the Queen and the Prince Consort at Dalkeith Palace in 1842, delegates from St Andrews and Glasgow, but apparently not Aberdeen, also took part in the ceremony. Side by side with the practice of addressing the Sovereign and his Consort was developing the practice of conferring 'by acclamation' honorary degrees upon members of the royal family, for example, the Dukes of Clarence and Sussex in 1820 and the Prince Consort in 1842.

The University was by this time in fairly regular communication with a whole range of ministers and their departments. Appeals for funds were frequently addressed to the lords of the Treasury. The help of the Colonial Office was invoked successfully in securing specimens for the Natural History museum and that of the Board of Customs for special privileges in importing them as well as exemption from customs duties. Memorials were constantly going to the Home Secretary and the Law officers of the Crown about legislation which adversely affected the interests of the University or might do so if certain bills before Parliament became law. In return ministers sometimes asked the advice of the Senatus, for example, about the cost of transforming the sinecure Regius Chair of Practical Astronomy into a going concern by supplying the necessary instruments to make observations. Draft legislation on new constitutions for the Scottish universities or the regulation of medical education and practice by government was occasionally submitted to the Senatus and their opinions invited – and sometimes listened to.

Among these subjects any differentiation in the treatment accorded by parliament to Scottish and English universities was bitterly resented. Melbourne had to promise to extend to the Scottish universities the long-standing privileges in regard to militia service enjoyed by Oxford and Cambridge. Edinburgh waged a long campaign to secure from the commissioners of excise the drawback on paper allowed to the English universities. But the most important of these controversies was over the representation of the Scottish universities in Parliament. In 1831 the Senatus petitioned both houses of Parliament in favour of this, while the agitation for parliamentary reform was at its height, thus separating itself from the Toryism of Wellington and Peel and clearly aligning itself as in the earlier eighteenth century with the Whig party. Dr Christison raised the question again in 1853 and was supported by the Edinburgh Senatus as well as by Marischal College, Aberdeen. Again in 1857, at the request of the Association of Graduates, the Senatus sent a memorial on this subject to Lord Palmerston, but it was not until 1867–8 that the grievance was at last remedied by the Second Reform Act.

On such occasions as these, it became the regular practice to send one or more professors to London to lobby ministers and, if necessary, to try to influence the attitude of the houses of Parliament. Macaulay, while MP for the city of Edinburgh, proved himself an energetic and powerful ally of the Edinburgh professors. One might have expected some indication that the two most distinguished alumni of Edinburgh in politics, Palmerston and Russell, both of them Prime Ministers in later life, had taken an active part in securing the interests of their *alma mater*. They may, in fact, have done so; but it is difficult to point to any specific occasion upon which their personal attitude or influence visibly brought advantage to the University.

The constitution of 1858, which is to be examined in the next chapter, deliberately strengthened the existing links between the University and the state. The new offices of chancellor and rector were normally filled by prominent politicians and each election came to be a tussle between the two political parties. This tendency was further encouraged by the introduction of university franchise in 1868. While professors individually continued to be keen politicians, the University as a corporation ceased to be either Whig, as it had been in the eighteenth, or Tory, as it had been in the first half of the nineteenth century. With commendable impartiality it conferred honorary degrees both on Gladstone in 1860 and on Disraeli seven years later. On the latter occasion 'political parties vied with one another in brotherly love' and at the banquet Disraeli replied to the principal toast 'with an address which lasted rather over two hours and a half, but which, nevertheless, seemed to fatigue no one'.

‹4›

The Struggle for
Reform

CONSTITUTIONAL REFORM

THE APPOINTMENT of the Royal Commision on the
Scottish Universities by a Tory government in 1826 was due to
the quarrel between the town council of Edinburgh and the
professors of the Tounis College; but it has a much wider significance.
The Age of Reform had dawned. The universities were ceasing to be
regarded as privileged corporations, perpetuating themselves by co-
option, and ultimately dependent upon the Crown and the church.

While the Commissioners were intent upon increasing the practical
effects of control by the Crown, they played down the historic connection between the church and the universities. In their opinion the
Scottish universities 'possess scarcely any ecclesiastical feature, except
that they have a certain number of professors for the purpose of
teaching theology, in the same manner as other sciences are taught'.
This was certainly an understatement, which deliberately ignored
the statutory tests imposed upon all professors elect by the legislation
of Queen Anne's reign. It ignored also the more ancient right of the

ministers of Edinburgh to a voice in the choice of professors. When a determined effort was made by the Presbytery of Edinburgh to enforce these tests in 1805, at a time when the ministers were attempting to intervene in the choice of a professor of Mathematics, the Senatus retorted that their members were always ready 'to do what the laws of the State and of the Church prescribe', but pointed out that no professor had been called upon to take the tests for half a century. And to judge by the Senate records a mere handful of professors did take the tests in the following half-century. The spasmodic and occasional attempts of the Edinburgh Presbytery to recover a voice in the exercise of town-council patronage of Chairs was equally futile, being brushed aside by the Court of Session in a manner that can only be described as contemptuous.

The 1826 Commission's Report, in general, foreshadows clearly the later developments which made the universities state agencies, charged with responsibility to Parliament, and bound to play the part assigned to them in what was slowly and painfully becoming a national system of education. A minor indication of this process of change was the admission, without taking the customary oaths, of a practising Jew to graduate MD in 1828.

The final Report of the Commissioners, published in 1831, was based on a thorough examination of most aspects of university life and organisation. The universities must be brought and kept up to date, they must be kept in tune with public opinion and they must be efficiently managed. This triple task required the transfer of supreme authority in each university to a University Court, on which the professional and lay elements would be separately represented and, it was hoped, reconciled. The proposal that the graduates should have a voice in the election of one of the members of Court was the first recognition at Edinburgh that graduates had any right to share in the government of their University. This Court would take over the whole direction of the University hitherto shared in practice by the town council and the professors. So anxious were the professors to get rid of town-council supervision, that they approved in principle the control and direction of the University by 'a Court of intelligent and well-educated persons', subject to the proviso that it should not have power to dismiss or suspend any professor.

The Whig governments in power in the 1830s were preoccupied with major problems and were at the best half-hearted in carrying out by legislation the recommendations of their reforming Tory predecessors. As soon as Peel returned to power in 1841, the Senatus urged upon the Home Secretary the immediate establishment of a rectorial court, and begged the government to provide salaries for those professors who were no longer being paid by the bankrupt town council. Constitutional reform and financial security had become aspects of a single problem, which was further complicated by the Disruption of 1843.

Members of the Free Church of Scotland could not honestly make the declarations legally required before they could be inducted as professors. Only a minority of Scotsmen were now eligible for university Chairs in their own country. A law originally passed to exclude Episcopalians was being applied to exclude Presbyterian dissenters, while Episcopalians were being exempted. As early as 1848 Christison carried in the Senate a resolution favouring amendment of the tests, on condition that 'the Christian and Protestant character' of the University should be maintained by the requirement that holders of Theological Chairs must be ministers or licentiates of the Church of Scotland. Moncreiff's Act of 1853 (16 and 17 Victoria c. 89 section 2) substituted for most professors an innocuous declaration in place of the stringent requirements of Anne's legislation and removed the possibility of injustice to individuals: the Free Churchman McDougall, who had been appointed by the town council to the Chair of Moral Philosophy in 1847, could not be inducted until Moncreiff's Act came into force. But the Act did have the unfortunate effect of increasing a dangerous tendency: electors to Chairs often preferred a less qualified candidate of their own denomination to a better qualified candidate of another denomination.

Amongst the other reforms proposed by the Commission of 1826 were a revision of the curriculum in various faculties and changes in the recognition, teaching, and grouping of academic subjects. In the 1850s these problems were brought into prominence by the Association for the Improvement and Extension of the Scottish Universities, which was controlled by Edinburgh graduates and had its headquarters in Edinburgh. Its leading spirit was James Lorimer, junior, later professor of Public Law. Apart from championing the rights of graduates to take part in the government of the University, Lorimer was not much interested in constitutional reform: the government must provide money to found new Chairs, increase existing professorial salaries and provide retiring allowances, develop the tutorial system of instruction, and appoint external examiners to keep up standards.

47. Professor James Lorimer; from the Tercentenary Photographic Album, 1883.

In spite of Sir William Hamilton's celebrated attacks upon town-council patronage in the *Edinburgh Review* of 1834, the Senatus appear to have been willing to acquiesce in its continuance and it was proposed to be retained in the Universities (Scotland) Bill, as submitted by Lord Advocate Inglis to the House of Commons for first reading.* When members of the house showed hostility, often based on ignorance, to town-council patronage, Inglis hurriedly added a section which

* See D. B. Horn, The Universities (Scotland) Act of 1858 in *Univ. of Edin. Journal,* Spring 1959, pp. 169–99, for a fuller treatment of the Act of 1858 and the movement which led up to it.

would preserve the rights of, for example, the Faculty of Advocates, but would deprive the council of its patronage as well as of its right of supervision and control. Finally a compromise solution, the transfer of town-council patronage to an *ad hoc* body, the curators of patronage, with a permanent majority of town council over university representatives of four to three, was achieved by the 1858 Act and has worked surprisingly well in practice. The last exercise of patronage by the town council was to appoint the distinguished scientist and Free Churchman, Sir David Brewster, as the first lay principal of the University. This was possible because of another clause of the 1858 Act by which the offices of principal at Edinburgh, Glasgow, and St Andrews were no longer to be considered as Chairs in Theology as they had been by Moncreiff's Act of 1853.

Unfortunately, the curators continued to be affected by improper influences much as the town council had been. Brewster himself described one of the early elections as 'disgraceful' and in 1864 Lister's application for the Chair of Surgery was rejected. In the General Council a motion was even carried to transfer all patronage exercised by the curators to the University Court; but matters improved when the town councillors appointed to the board of curators such men as William Chambers and occasionally elected outsiders like Lord Gifford, founder of the Gifford Lectures. The University representatives were nearly all judges and other successful advocates, although Gladstone himself served for two terms, and from 1877 it became customary to have the principal as one of the University's curators. If the town council had been too much influenced by the ecclesiastical connections of candidates, as when a certain councillor asked a puzzled English candidate for a Chair 'are ye a jined member o' onie boadie?', the curators seem to have been too inclined to enquire whether he was a Liberal or a Conservative.

Apart from its majority voice in patronage, the town council, under the 1858 Act, continued to share in the government of the University through its two representatives on the University Court of eight members. Indeed the influence of the town council upon Court decisions, owing to the fact that its assessors were necessarily resident in Edinburgh, may have been greater than the proportion of its representatives to the whole Court would suggest. The other 'lay'

48. Principal Sir David Brewster; from the Tercentenary Photographic Album, 1883.

STUDENTS!

Do not be imposed upon by the flood of printed trash with which Mr Moncreiff's supporters are deluging the University in the hope of securing a party victory.

Mr RUSKIN'S qualifications are simply these :

1. He is the finest living writer of the English language. He will therefore be able to give you a stirring address, more worthy of the literary renown of the University than any heaped up verbiage of legal and theological hair-splitters.

2. He will make a worthy successor to Mr Carlyle, as he belongs to the same open, honest, and independent British school of writers.

No one who has read the "Stones of Venice" can fail to perceive his just claims on an educated constituency.

49. A handbill issued by Ruskin's supporters in the Rectorial Election of 1868.

members of the Court were the rector, who was named as its chairman and was to be elected by the matriculated students; an assessor to be nominated by the rector, on the clear assumption that the rector would not himself regularly attend meetings; an assessor to be elected by the newly instituted General Council; and an assessor to be nominated by the chancellor, who was not himself to be a member of the Court. The professional members of the Court were to be the principal and one assessor to be elected by the Senatus; and the inadequacy of this representation in numbers, if not in quality, soon became matter of complaint among members of Senatus. It was expressly laid down that no University principal or professor could be elected as rector or assessor, except in the case of the assessor to be elected by the Senatus.

Above the Court was the chancellor, to be elected for life by the General Council. Lord Brougham, now an extinct volcano, became the first chancellor and was succeeded in 1868 by the draftsman of the new constitution for the University, John Inglis. Presumably contrary to the intentions of the 1858 Act, the first two rectors, W. E. Gladstone and Thomas Carlyle, were certainly men of greater national reputation than the first two chancellors.

Hardly less important than the establishment of the University Court and the creation of what were, in the case of Edinburgh, really new offices of equal dignity and power, was the institution of the General Council. There had been agreement amongst University reformers that some such institution was desirable, even necessary. The case was perhaps best put by Lorimer. It would enhance the value of graduation,* give the graduates the feelings of a corporate body, 'introduce a new element of youth and freshness into the government of the universities, which would have the effect at once of controlling the selfish views with which professors, and the ignorance and bigotry with which municipal patrons, have so often been charged'. Finally, membership of the General Council would keep graduates in touch with the University and encourage those who became 'prosperous and influential' to advance its interests and contribute to its endowment. Other and more politically minded reformers added the argument that the government, which had refused to create a university franchise in Scotland for the benefit of a handful of professors,

---

* The institution of graduation *in absentia* in the Faculty of Medicine in 1839 would seem to be the first sign of the increasing importance now being attached to degrees.

ministers, and schoolmasters, would change its mind if the practice of graduation became universal and large General Councils resulted. Partly to secure this object, membership of the Council was not at first limited to graduates; other alumni were to be admitted to membership if they had attended certain courses of study for prescribed periods.

No serious attempt was made to enable this body to play the part of a parliament in the new University constitution. Their powers were merely 'to take into their consideration all questions affecting the well-being and prosperity of the University and to make representations from time to time on such questions to the University Court, who shall consider the same, and return to the Council their deliverance thereon'. Nor was their approval necessary to enable the Court to carry out its plans for 'improvements' in the University. The powers exercised by Convocation in the English universities were deliberately withheld from the Scottish General Councils; apart from electing a chancellor for life and an assessor on the Court for a term of years, their function was limited to the proffering of advice–solicited or unsolicited–to the Court.

To establish its independence of the town council, the Senatus had been driven to accept what was clearly a position of dependence upon the Court. Not only were its functions, as defined by the Act, in effect limited to routine regulation of the teaching and discipline of the University and administration of its properties and revenues, but the exercise by Senatus of these functions would be 'subject to the control and review of the University Court'. To the Court also was assigned the initiative in effecting 'improvements in the internal affairs of the University'. While such improvements required the sanction of the chancellor, they had merely to be communicated to the Senatus and 'submitted to the University Council for their consideration' before being put into effect. Moreover, the Court was entrusted with judicial powers over the individual professors. In particular, it could censure, suspend, or deprive any principal or professor–these royal powers had hitherto been delegated only to special commissioners from time to time, but were now permanently entrusted to the Court, subject only to approval by Her Majesty in Council in each case. Some professors certainly thought, as Burke had remarked in another connection, that the medicine of the constitution was in danger of becoming its daily food.

At first the sovereignty of the Court was masked by another feature of the 1858 Act, borrowed by Inglis from the earlier Acts for the reform of the English universities. This was the establishment of a body of executive commissioners with very full powers to enquire into every aspect of the Scottish universities and carry through by ordinances any reforms that they thought desirable, subject only to their ordinances being submitted to Parliament and approved by Her Majesty in Council. The commissioners appointed by the Act may be divided into three categories; peers, judges, and members of the House of Commons who had been prominent in the debates on the 1858 Act. This was to be a temporary arrangement. Once the Augean stables of the Scottish universities had been cleansed and the parliamentary grants allocated to purposes approved by the Commissioners for each university, then the executive commission would come to an end. When the Commissioners' powers expired at the end of December, 1862, the University Courts, each in its own sphere, added to their executive supremacy and judicial functions the right to alter or revoke the ordinances which had been made by the Commissioners, subject to the written consent of the chancellor of the university concerned and the approval of Her Majesty in Council.

CURRICULAR AND ADMINISTRATIVE REFORMS

The basic ideas of the University Commissioners of 1826 on the proper constitution of a university had been translated into fact by the Act of 1858; but neither the Commissioners of 1826 nor those of 1858 were so foolish as to imagine that a mere change of constitution would cure all the evils and remove all the difficulties. While not blind to the advantages of the elastic eighteenth-century system, which allowed most students to choose their subjects and plan their own course of study, the Commissioners of 1826 had been determined to institute, or rather to restore, 'a regular and systematic course of study' in Arts, to be taken by students who aimed at university honours or whose future profession required them to take 'a complete University curriculum'. They had been anxious also to render 'the method of communicating instruction more efficient'.

Their recommended curriculum had been extremely conservative, as to subjects to be included; but they had insisted on the need for repeated attendances in successive years on the classical and mathematical classes. They had also made it clear that the work of the philosophical classes should not consist merely of formal lectures, as was then the practice at Edinburgh, but should include written and oral examinations for one hour at each two-hourly meeting of these classes. They had been particularly concerned to raise the standard of instruction in Latin, Greek, and Mathematics, proposing to institute preliminary examinations in these subjects for exemption from the first course. These examinations must be conducted not by interested professors but by independent examiners, and, in the case of the two larger universities, provision must be made for the appointment of two assistants, one in Latin and another in Greek, to help the professors. Any attempt to establish a system of college tutorships they had considered undesirable. A new Chair of Political Economy was proposed for Edinburgh and this subject, along with Chemistry, should be added to the Arts curriculum. Rhetoric should be reunited to Logic. Universal History should be taught but not as a compulsory subject for Arts degrees. The Regius professor of Practical Astronomy had died recently 'having been only once or twice in the University for many years before his death': the Commissioners thought no successor to him should be appointed until an observatory attached to the University had been provided.

Competition should be stimulated by establishing prizes in each class and making the attainment of 'academical honours' an object of ambition, particularly for upper-class students and for those intended for the Church or the Bar. There would be strict examination, not by the professors but by examiners to be appointed by Senatus, of all candidates for the BA or MA. Candidates who so desired could enter for the BA with honours and if successful would be placed either with 'honourable distinction' or 'with the highest class of honours'. The latter category of honours might be 'taken either in classical or scientific attainments' and apparently also in philosophy. The MA degree would be taken at least a year later than the BA, after attendance on and examination in three additional subjects, Natural History, Chemistry, and Political Economy. The 'principal examination' for the master's degree would, however, be 'in any branch of literature, philosophy, or science' selected by the candidate.

Turning to the Faculty of Divinity, the Commissioners of 1826 had expressed their dissatisfaction with the existing arrangements authorised by the General Assembly. They drew up a model curriculum, proposed to regulate the order in which classes were to be taken and suggested means of ensuring the regular attendance of all students. A new Chair of Biblical Criticism was required at Edinburgh and a new degree, Bachelor of Divinity, should be introduced as an 'object of ambition'. Similarly in the Law Faculty, a regular curriculum was prescribed, although no suggestion of a degree in Law below that of doctor was made. Conveyancing should be compulsory and the sine-cure Chair of Public Law should be abolished.

In Medicine, the Commissioners had strongly supported the need for a preliminary examination to be conducted by the examiners for degrees in Arts, covering Classics, Mathematics, and Natural Philosophy. The medical curriculum should ideally extend over five years, but the Commissioners did not recommend that this should come into operation at once. Anatomy and Surgery should be taught by different professors. Practical Chemistry, Practical Pharmacy, and Midwifery and Diseases of Women and Children, but not Medical Jurisprudence, should be recognised as compulsory subjects. Subject to safeguards, extra-mural teaching by private lecturers should be recognised. While making their usual recommendations, intended to secure regular attendance by students on medical classes, the Commissioners reluctantly left the conduct of degree examinations to the Medical professors. The examination should, however, be conducted in English and theses should no longer be required, though any candidate who desired to do so might submit one either in Latin or in English.

Though basically conservative in approach, and specifically anxious to avoid the assimilation of the Scottish to the English University system, these recommendations clearly foreshadowed the shape of things to come. The provisional views of the Commissioners of 1826 on the *curricula* were submitted piecemeal to the Senatus in the winter of 1828–9 and it is possible to trace their effect on subsequent decisions of that body and its constituent faculties.

In Arts new regulations for the MA degree were drawn up in 1831 and these specified the content and standard of the examination in each of the traditional seven subjects in a way that had not been done for more than a century. Whereas set books were to be the basis of examination in Classics and Mathematics, the degree examinations in the philosophical branches were to be based on the lectures given by the various professors. About the same time J. D. Forbes borrowed from the English universities for use in degree examinations the new technique of written question papers, supplemented by the old practice of oral discussions between examiner and candidates. Forbes's colleagues, Hamilton and Kelland, objected to what they regarded as over-emphasis on written questions; but in April 1836 six candidates who had survived a three-day examination in Classics, Mathematics, and Philosophy, were recommended by the Faculty of Arts for the degree of MA. Their names were arranged in a strict order of merit— as indeed they would also have been in the early seventeenth century.

The real novelty of the new procedure was the arrangement by which candidates could take the examination in Classics at the end of the third year and have the result carried forward to the final-year examination. This is the beginning of the process by which ordinary degrees could be taken step by step by a process of accumulation. Hamilton then began, on his own authority but in accordance with the recommendations of the 1826 Commissioners, to examine such students as were prepared to read extra books on philosophy not required for the ordinary degree, and, if they satisfied his tests, to award them 'philosophical honours'. Thus was taken another step along the academic path which led to the differentiation between ordinary and honours degrees in the Arts Faculty.

In 1842 the Arts Faculty proposed regulations to revive the BA degree on the lines recommended by the Commissioners of 1826, and, subject to the deletion of written examination questions, this was approved by Senatus. Thus in many ways the Commissioners' Report was being implemented at Edinburgh by energetic and enlightened professors such as J. D. Forbes and Sir William Hamilton. On the other hand, Hamilton's refusal for more than ten years to take part in examining candidates for degrees, on the ground that the Faculty of Arts had on one occasion recommended for the degree of MA two candidates whom he thought completely ignorant of logic and meta-physics, would certainly not have been approved by the Commis-sioners, who would doubtless have regarded his behaviour as additional proof that some kind of University Court with superintendence over the professors was necessary in the interests of other professors as well as of the public.

Some, but not all, of the Commission's recommendations regarding the medical curriculum were incorporated in the new statutes of 1833. In 1837 the Senatus decided to recognise lectures given at such institutions as University College, London, provided that they had been recognised by the Metropolitan University of London. It was hoped to secure in return recognition from the University of London for the courses of lectures given at Edinburgh University. Not until 1845 was this recognition extended to courses given at London Teach-ing Hospitals. We may perhaps see also the influence of the Royal

Commission when the Medical Faculty began in 1838 to star the names of candidates for the doctorate in medicine who received the particular approbation of the Faculty.

In 1835 the Faculty of Divinity asked permission of the Senatus to confer the BD degree and promised to keep it a select and reputable degree. Approval was given by Senatus and all candidates were required to have previously taken the degree of MA and the subjects (Theology, Church History, and Oriental Languages) and content of the examination were adjusted in 1837. When a degree in Music was instituted in 1847, all candidates were required to have reached BA standard before beginning the course.

When the government proposed in 1836 to appoint by Act of Parliament a Board of Royal Visitors to regulate the Scottish universities, the Lord Advocate was ready to allow the Senatus to frame in the first place 'all regulations with regard to the curriculum of study and the discipline of the College', subject to an appeal by interested parties to the Board of Visitors. Although the Commissioners did not themselves recommend it, they would undoubtedly have approved, as a means of raising the value of medical degrees, 'the adoption of an academical costume' for doctors of medicine in 1843, followed in 1844 by the adoption of a cap borrowed from Cambridge, and an arrangement by which graduands in Medicine were required either to buy for themselves or to hire from the Albion Cloth Company, at a charge of five shillings, the proper costume in which to appear at medical graduations.

In some ways the most important suggestion by the Commissioners of 1826 on the Arts curriculum was the recognition that if standards in Classics and Mathematics were to be effectively raised an entrance examination of some kind must be instituted for each class. Here again this was no novelty, but rather a return under new conditions to seventeenth-century practice. While Latin and Mathematics were adequately taught in many Scottish schools and candidates who came up badly equipped in these subjects usually had only themselves to blame, Greek was hardly a school subject at all. Indeed the eighteenth- and early nineteenth-century professors of Greek, such as Dunbar in 1820, looked upon the teaching of Greek at Edinburgh's High School as an abuse and a manifest infringement of their monopoly. Traditionally, the first University Greek class began with instruction in the Greek alphabet and not many Edinburgh students spent more than six months in studying the language; those who had taken it at the

High School sometimes omitted it on the ground that they already knew more Greek than the other students would know at the end of the first University session.

To their credit it was the town council which, on appointing Blackie to the Greek Chair in 1852, tried to end this long-standing scandal by instituting a compulsory preliminary examination for admission to the Greek class. The Senatus approved and went further. They arranged to appoint and pay out of the Reid fund under their control, College tutors, both in Greek and Latin, to bring students who were likely to fail in the preliminary examinations up to the required standard. The conduct of this examination was at first very lenient. Of five students who were reported to the Senatus as not quite fit for admission to the Greek class, one was at once admitted and the others 'put under training for a fortnight'. Since Blackie's competitor, Lushington, persisted in teaching the merest elements of Greek at Glasgow, Blackie was prepared in 1855 to accept an examination based on 'any one book of the Anabasis or any one of the gospels'. Although the Senatus preferred an alternative scheme proposed by Pillans for a preliminary examination at the beginning of the second year both in Greek and Latin, Blackie persuaded the town council to continue the existing entrance examination for the first Greek class. In 1855–6 eighteen students were allowed to defer taking this examination until February, being taught meantime in a separate class by the Greek tutor, and in the end only three were rejected.

Pillans then applied to have a grant from the Reid fund so that he could adopt the same procedure in admitting students to the Humanity class. A similar request was made by the department of Mathematics, while the professor of Rhetoric wanted a grant to pay an assistant to revise the class exercises of his students. Finally in 1857 the Senatus approved a general resolution that it was expedient to appoint tutors in Humanity, Greek, and Mathematics and possibly in other Arts classes. The office of University assistant, as distinct from that of personal assistant to a professor, had accidentally come into existence. Logic was added to the subjects in which University assistantships existed in 1857, presumably because it was regarded as a compulsory introduction to the other philosophical studies.

The institution of these University assistantships was merely one of many methods proposed, and as a rule adopted, by the University, in accordance with the recommendations of the 1826 Commission, to make the existing system of instruction more efficient. It should,

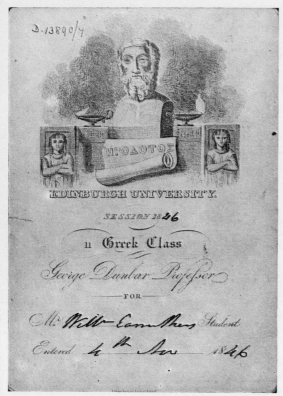

50. A class card issued to William Carruthers in 1846.

however, be realised that most of these reforms were merely developments of, or in some cases a return to, earlier University practice.
Such were the stipulations designed to ensure regular attendance on
classes, the due performance of written work, and the testing of
progress by frequent written and oral examinations. Professors must
not grant certificates to students who had not deserved them; and it
was the Commissioners of 1826 who drew up the formula which is the
basis of the present DP certificate, required before a student can offer
himself for examination for any degree. The Commissioners were
determined to root out the ancient practice by which careless and
good-natured professors issued certificates to all and sundry. This
had had the incidental result, that it was often unsatisfactory students
who took degrees in Arts, since good students preferred to depend on

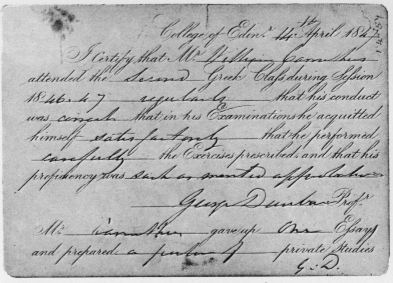

51. 'DP', which appears on the back of the Greek class card (p. 165).

letters of recommendation from their professors, which were in higher esteem than degrees secured virtually without examination and often *in absentia*.

Progress was also made along other lines suggested by the Commissioners. It was not enough to institute, or try to raise the standards of degrees in different faculties. The Commissioners set an exaggerated value on prize essays and themselves provided funds to institute one such competition. A few individuals about this time also contributed funds for this purpose. The Senatus brought what influence it could upon the town council to extend the system of prizes traditionally awarded in certain classes to the best students. A few professors even provided such prizes for their classes out of their own pockets.

For a few years such competitions were so popular that large numbers of students subscribed small sums to form a fund administered by the Senatus out of which prizes for essays could be awarded. Many such essays were published in collections such as *The Edinburgh University Souvenir*, published in 1835, and *The Edinburgh Academic Annual*, published in 1840. Few of them can have enhanced the reputation of the University for scholarship. The entries for such prize essays as were announced soon dropped to a mere handful. Sometimes the prize could not be awarded at all. The craze for prize-essay writing was manifestly on the decline, even although the Senatus sometimes threw in an honorary MA as an additional inducement to competitors. In the long run more important than the prize essay was the institution of assistantships which, as Blackie pointed out, did something to enable 'an ambitious Scotch graduate . . . to ripen into the stature of a finished scholar' and keep him alive in the meantime.

Parallel with the measures intended to raise entrance standards in all faculties, to increase competition amongst students, and to persuade the majority of them to aim at higher standards in working for the old and new degrees, was the gradual recognition by the learned professions in Scotland that the possession of a degree, or in some cases attendance at University classes for a prescribed period, should be the normal test, supplemented if necessary by professional examinations, for admission to the profession. All along the Church of Scotland had required not a degree but attendance upon a full course in philosophy for all entrants to the ministry. In 1855 the Faculty of Advocates adopted new rules of admission which made the MA degree the normal test of non-professional attainments. Many of the applicants for honorary MAs in the first half of the nineteenth century were schoolmasters who found that their lack of an Arts degree was a drawback to their professional advancement, or a hindrance to securing recognition of their scholastic status furth of Scotland.

Another powerful influence was the introduction of appointment to government posts by competitive examination in place of nomination. This began with East Indian cadetships in the 1850s and soon extended to many appointments in the home civil service. There was an outcry when Scottish candidates at first did badly in such examinations and this certainly contributed both to raise standards and broaden the curriculum in Arts. And it was in this period that the ancient tradition became firmly established that the ambitious Scottish schoolboy, before beginning a course of professional study at the university, should first take an Arts degree or at least demonstrate his ability to do so by reaching the prescribed standard in some of the required subjects.

FINANCE

Beyond pointing out the utter inadequacy of the remuneration of the principal and the professors in the Faculty of Divinity, the Commissioners of 1826 had little to say about the University's finances. They accepted more or less at its face value the evidence submitted by the

officials of the corporation which showed that the revenues appropriated specifically to the University were quite inadequate to its annual
upkeep. The officials reckoned that on an average, between 1775 and
1825, there was a deficiency of over £250 a year, even taking into
account occasional capital payments received by the town council in
the form of legacies or sales of property, such as the teinds of Dun-
barnie in 1820. Though the real values of the salaries attached to
most of the Chairs had declined, the Commissioners felt that those
professors who attracted reasonable audiences were adequately remunerated by fees. Chairs to which this simple arithmetical rule did
not apply should be abolished at the first opportunity. So should all
sinecure professorships, such as the Chair of Public Law, and the
salaries attached to these Chairs could then be used to better purpose.

So far as the Senatus was concerned it had in 1800 only two sources
of revenue worth mention: (1) the matriculation fees collected from
students which were, according to ancient tradition, expended mainly
on the Library; and (2) fees payable on graduation, which were
inconsiderable except in Medicine, where they were mostly divided
amongst the examiners for the MD degree. A third source was indeed
added after the Commission had reported in 1831 – the income on
substantial bequests to the University from two military alumni,
Generals Reid (1838) and Straton (1840). Before the Reid bequest
became payable on the death of the general's daughter the Senatus
had already borrowed £5,500 in anticipation of future payment; and
attempts to apply the moneys actually received to what the Senatus
regarded as the most pressing needs of the University, without over-
nice respect for the wishes of the testator, soon involved them in
protracted legal actions.

The Senatus could hardly be expected to share the complacency of
the Commissioners of 1826 on University finance, especially as the
financial situation deteriorated markedly in the years after 1831. In
1835 a memorial from the Senatus begging for government help was
brusquely rejected by the Lords of the Treasury. By this time the
bankruptcy of the town council had been publicly acknowledged,
and the town's creditors refused in 1836 to accept a scheme of accommodation which would have secured something from the wreck for
the University. In 1837 to make matters worse, the Ale duty, out of
which the salaries of several professors were paid, finally expired. The
Senatus were not easily discouraged and continued to press their
claims upon the government in further memorials and by sending a

deputation to London. In a memorable phrase Thomas Chalmers asserted that the University could only be saved from disaster by 'the helping hand of government'. This in 1839 took the form of a grant of £2,500 a year from the revenues of Leith harbour towards the University and schools of Edinburgh, which was quite inadequate, especially as the town council by this arrangement was freed from the obligation to pay bursaries on various mortifications administered by them. These were henceforth to be payable out of this government grant.

Thus the forties were hungry within the University as well as outside. Professorial salaries were usually years in arrear; some were not paid at all. Peel refused to give more help in 1845 and in one session, according to the principal, two Edinburgh professors were forced by starvation to migrate to St Andrews. It was financial need as much as its quarrel with the town council which forced the Senatus to accept the supremacy of the University Court as a condition of securing more adequate financial support from the government. The increased Government grant provided by the Act of 1858 was merely a first step to a sounder system of University finance. It is characteristic of the Victorian age of self-help that the major contributions to solving the University's cumulative financial problems came in the next generation from generous private benefactions and a substantial growth of income from fees for tuition and graduation.

The Transition to the Modern University 1858 – 1889

THE ADMINISTRATIVE AND FINANCIAL REFORMS OF THE COMMISSIONERS OF 1858

WHEREAS THE other Scottish universities for various reasons resented the passing of the Universities (Scotland) Act of 1858, it was warmly welcomed at Edinburgh. As the new principal, Sir David Brewster, pointed out, the Act greatly increased the powers and privileges of Edinburgh professors, graduates, and students, and all three categories were eager to enter the promised land. The Act itself provided a bare framework and entrusted to a body of executive commissioners the thankless tasks of elaborating the details of a new Constitution; they allocated to Edinburgh its share of the increased government grant to the Scottish universities and decided how this inadequate sum could best be spent. They also prescribed *curricula* for the various faculties, adjusting the detailed regulations for graduation, fixing fees payable by students and salaries payable to professors, introducing rules for retiring allowances for professors, and superintending all the administrative and financial arrangements for the transfer of the College from the control of the town council. It says much for the ability and tact of the Commissioners and particularly of their chairman, John Inglis, that it had accomplished these tasks by the end of 1862 without arousing a universal howl of execration from all those aggrieved by its decisions.

As illustrative of the importance of the Commissioners' decisions on the constitution of the University, it is worth mentioning that these included the determination of the conditions upon which alumni who had not graduated could, during a transitional period, be admitted to membership of the General Council, and, of more permanent importance, the provision that the General Council could not adjourn its meetings from day to day, and that all members of the council resident in the United Kingdom should have a postal vote in the election of chancellor or assessor. More important still it was the Commissioners who awarded to the principal the right, in the absence of the rector, to preside over the University Court and, when acting as chairman, to exercise a casting as well as a deliberative vote. And it was the Commissioners who recommended to the Crown the procedure by which, before any of their ordinances so far as applicable to one of the universities, could be altered or revoked by its university Court, the proposed changes must first have been communicated to the other universities. In practice, and this was foreseen by the Commissioners, the adoption of this rule made change more difficult and helped to preserve 'the uniformity which, in a great measure, we have succeeded in establishing'. In insisting upon what they had done to secure uniformity, the Commissioners were probably answering in advance Gladstonian criticism of their failure to make any progress towards the establishment of a national University of Scotland as provided by the Act.

When the Commissioners turned to the financial affairs of the University, they discovered that the Act of 1858 had not effectively transferred the buildings and site to the Senatus Academicus. This necessitated the passing in 1861 of the Edinburgh University Property Arrangement Act. Moreover the town council, indignant at the loss of its control over the University, tried to secure permission from the Lords of the Treasury to transfer from the University to the High School £125 a year, which formed part of the annuity secured on the revenues of the port of Leith and allocated by Act of Parliament in 1838 to the support of the College and schools of Edinburgh. Although they used the arguments that any reduction in the annuity from Leith harbour would have to be made good out of public moneys to the

University ('the poorest, although the most numerously attended of the Universities of Scotland'), and that the corporation was selfishly seeking to reduce the cost of a local educational institution to themselves, the University Commissioners had finally to accept a compromise which reduced the University's share of the annuity from £2,210 to £2,170 and increased the schools' share correspondingly from £290 to £330. Nearly £400 of the College share was, however, required to pay bursaries which, previous to 1838, had been payable out of College funds administered by the town council, so that the free income from the Leith annuity was reduced to £1,770 approximately.

Worse still, in order to secure a permanent division of the Leith annuity between the University and the town council, the Commissioners were forced to give up the University's claim to what the town council itself called the 'College revenue proper'. This consisted of (1) the ancient mortcloth dues, now greatly diminished, which the corporation contended were wholly required to maintain the burial grounds in the city; (2) ground annuals, feu duties, and teinds producing a net income of just over £40 a year, and the teinds likely to be further reduced by future augmentations of ministers' stipends; (3) tack duties or rents of property in North College Street amounting to £44 net *per annum* which would be drastically curtailed when this property was partly demolished and the street widened to improve the access to the new Industrial museum to be built to the west of the University; and (4) annuities on bonds representing sums received by the sale of the patronage of Currie and Wemyss and Fala churches, £54. It was in vain that the University Commissioners pointed out that the College had, in fact, received a revenue of above £80 a year from the mortcloth dues alone for the past fifteen years, and that, in all, revenues amounting in 1861 to £230 a year would be transferred from the University to the town council, apart from the additional £40 a year extorted by the town council from the University's share of the Leith annuity. All claims to these revenues on behalf of the College were rejected by the Lords of the Treasury and the Edinburgh University Property Arrangement Act awarded them to the town council, possibly with the idea that the town council deserved compensation for the transfer of the College buildings and site to the University. It is easy to understand the attitude of the town council at the time. Looking back, one can only regret that the divorce of College and council after nearly 300 years of married life was not marked by a single trace of good feeling, let alone generosity, on the part of the corporation.

In 1861 the University began a new chapter in its history, stripped of nearly all its old endowments, and dependent financially on its fee income from various sources, government grants, and its share in the revenues of Leith harbour. To these sources should be added the income on the two bequests which had escaped the clutches of the town council. While General Reid's bequest was largely devoted to the Chair of Music, the surplus amounting to £800 or £900 a year was available for general University purposes. From the other bequest by Sir Joseph Straton, about £500 a year was also available for general purposes. While one must acquit the town council of deliberate embezzlement of the funds entrusted to it by pious benefactors of the Tounis College, the final result of its management of the College finances over a period of nearly 300 years produced much the same result.

The Commissioners had now to allocate the available revenue amongst a host of clamant needs. They felt impelled to raise professorial salaries on the principle that a whole time professor should receive £400–£500 a year,* while part-time professors in the Faculties of Law and Medicine, with other sources of income, should receive at least £200 a year. The Commissioners were favourably impressed by the work being done by assistants in the Faculties of Arts and Medicine and provided salaries for four in each of these Faculties to be attached to the Chairs most in need of assistance. The whole revenues of the University after deduction of certain preferential charges, mostly professorial salaries, were to constitute a General University Fund, out of which were to be met the current expenditure of the University, including the class expenses of particular professorships, the expenses of the Library, and such items as the salaries and wages of officers and servants and the cost of cleaning and heating the classrooms.

The Commissioners were gravely concerned about the maintenance of the University buildings and recommended that this should be undertaken by the government, acting through the Office of Works, as otherwise the buildings would probably be suffered 'to fall into

---

* The Commissioners of 1876 recommended an increase to £600 inclusive of class fees. In fact at this time (Session 1875–6) the professor of Anatomy received at least £2,245 after deduction of class expenses, whereas the professor of History's gross income was £264 10s.

disrepair or decay' owing to the lack of University funds. This recommendation was not accepted but it led, in 1869, to a government grant for this purpose of £500 a year. By this time the Senatus had adopted the enlightened practice of publishing yearly in the *Calendar* 'a statement showing the position of the funds and the income and expenditure of the University for the last financial year'. From these accounts it would appear that in every year from 1867 to 1876 maintenance and repair of University buildings and furnishings greatly exceeded the amount of the government grant and reached in 1876 a total of £766 19s. 9d.

CHANGES IN CURRICULA AND GRADUATION

The decisions of the 1858 Commissioners in regard to graduation in the various faculties determined the scholastic development of the Scottish universities for the rest of the nineteenth century. They were designed to secure uniformity so far as practicable and, by so doing, to raise academic standards and make Scottish degrees more respectable. In Arts the four-year course for the MA degree was to be maintained, but first-year students who took and passed a preliminary examination in Latin and Greek would be admitted to graduate at the end of the third year. Students who did not pass in these subjects, and also in Mathematics, must attend the junior course in each before admission to the graduating course. The Senatus Academicus of each university was to regulate the order in which the seven compulsory Arts classes were to be taken. The seven subjects, for degree examination purposes, were divided into three groups: (1) Latin and Greek; (2) Logic, Moral Philosophy, and English Literature; and (3) Mathematics and Natural Philosophy. As soon as he had attended the necessary courses, a student could present himself for final examination in any group and thus take the MA degree piecemeal. This would, the Commissioners believed, lead to 'a more accurate knowledge' of each subject, with a consequent raising of standards, than 'if the whole subjects of the course were embraced in one examination'. It should be noted that this piecemeal method of examination was already customary at Edinburgh and was not introduced there by the Commissioners.

Much more revolutionary in conception and consequences was the provision by which students who had already satisfied the examiners in each of the three groups could present themselves 'for further examination in any one or more of the four following departments, viz.–(1) Classical Literature, (2) Mental Philosophy . . . (3) . . . Pure Mathematics and Natural Philosophy; and (4) Natural Science'. While there were to be two classes of honours in the first three departments, there would be only one in Natural Science, where it was anticipated there would be few candidates. Though they acquitted the professors of 'undue laxity' in examining for degrees, the Commissioners provided for examinerships in each department of study recognised for honours and declared that they could be held only by members of one of the General Councils. The degree of MA was no longer to be conferred, as it frequently had been at Edinburgh, 'as an honorary distinction without examination', on the ground that academical degrees should not be conferred 'on persons who had not completed the ordinary course of study'.

The BA degree, which had been instituted by the Senatus at Edinburgh in 1842, was abolished. While emphasising the need for more prolonged and intensive study of Classics and Mathematics, the Commissioners affirmed their belief that the prominence assigned to philosophy 'in past times should in no degree be diminished'. English Language and Literature, as taught by Professor Aytoun at Edinburgh, was an essential part of a liberal education; but no other new subject could be admitted, with the doubtful exception of one Science, without damaging the standard of attainment in the traditional subjects by undue dispersion of the attention of candidates for the MA degree.

Believing as they did that any sudden innovation, compulsory on all students, 'would be attended with serious danger', the Commissioners rejected proposals to increase the length of the winter session or to adopt the English practice of three terms, divided by longish vacations at Christmas and Easter. Either reform would make it impossible for poor students to attend the Scottish universities; while those better-off should devote the long vacation to private study.

The object and the advantages of a University education are not confined to the instruction received within the class-room. Besides imparting information, the lectures of the Professors are intended, in a great measure, to guide and to stimulate private study, and for this the long vacation affords the best opportunity. The student is then enabled to revise, by himself and at leisure, the subjects of his University studies, and to consider more fully, and carry out to their legitimate conclusions, the principles which he has heard enunciated by his

Professors. The encouragement thus given to independent
thought has an importance not lightly to be disregarded.
Moreover, the long vacation could be used profitably for the study of
useful subjects, such as Natural Science, not included in the compulsory
degree curriculum. Indeed voluntary courses in such subjects might
be instituted by the universities during the summer.*

While the Commissioners were conservative in their approach to
graduation in Arts, their medical ordinances effected much more
radical changes. Although they made few alterations in the actual
curriculum, and regarded the competition of extra-mural teaching as
beneficial, as did their successors of 1876, they introduced, in place
of the MD degree, the new degree of MB as the basic medical qualification. And any medical student who had followed the normal curriculum, had passed the corresponding degree examinations, and had
submitted a thesis, could now obtain, by asking for it and paying the
prescribed fee, the degree of Master in Surgery. In 1881 the present
practice, by which the two degrees in Medicine and Surgery must be
taken at the same time, was introduced. The MD degree was retained
by the Commissioners of 1858 'as a mark of honour or distinction' as
a higher degree intended for consultants and specialists and to be
awarded on proof of knowledge of certain Arts subjects, such as Greek
and Natural Philosophy and also the submission of a thesis.

These changes were indeed forced upon the Commissioners by the
Medical Act of 1858 and the attitude of the medical and surgical
corporations to the universities. Had the Commissioners not introduced the new degree in Surgery 'every graduate desiring to practise
Surgery would have been obliged, in addition to his University degree,
to obtain a diploma from one of the surgical corporations'. The
substitution of the MB for the MD degree was intended to assimilate
the Scottish to the English system, as was probably inevitable with a
new Medical Act applicable to the United Kingdom. The commissioners believed that they had made arrangements which would ensure
that holders of the new degree of MB would 'possess qualifications
fully as high as those formerly required' for the MD. Therefore no
additional examination in Medicine should be required of candidates
for the MD who had already graduated MB, especially as such examination might be held to imply that bachelors of medicine 'had already

---

* These views were cordially endorsed by the University Commissioners
of 1876.

been admitted to practice with imperfect and insufficient knowledge'. Such candidates for the MD degree unless they were already masters of Arts were to be examined in Greek and other Arts subjects only. They must also have continued for two years after, taking the MB degree, medical or surgical studies or practice. Graduation with honours in Medicine and Surgery was instituted in 1865 and three years later the graduates with honours were divided into two classes. In 1866, while theses were no longer to be required from candidates for MB or CM, each candidate for the doctorate in Medicine had to submit a thesis on some branch of medical knowledge, which he had continued to study after graduating MB. Increased specialisation was furthered by the establishment of such hospitals as the Royal Hospital for Sick Children, founded in 1860 and known to generations of medical students as the 'Sick Kids'.

Having thus vindicated the just claims of the universities against the medical and surgical corporations, the Commissioners extracted from the Secretary of State for War an admission that Edinburgh medical men holding the new degrees in Medicine and Surgery were 'equally qualified in both branches with the graduates or licentiates of any other body or bodies to whom [under the Medical Act of 1858] the same privileges of practice belong, for commissions in the Army Medical service'. Further 'to increase the importance of the degrees, as well as to strengthen the public confidence in their high character', the Commissioners arranged to associate with the Medical professors three examiners for degrees in Medicine, to be remunerated out of public funds. Fees for examining, which had hitherto been shared by the Medical professors, were henceforth to be paid to the General University Fund.

In dealing with the Faculty of Law, the Commissioners revived the Chair of Public Law, so long a sinecure, and required its holder to deliver lectures on International Law. Having rejected the claim that History should become a compulsory course for the Arts degree, the Commissioners transferred the History Chair to the Faculty of Law and ordained that the professor should teach Constitutional Law and History. The professors of Civil Law and Scots Law were also required to deliver courses of lectures during the summer session, in addition to conducting their existing winter classes. Thus at Edinburgh, alone of the Scottish universities, a student could now obtain 'complete instruction in the various departments of Law'. It remained to draw up regulations for the non-honorary degree in Law, the LLB, which the Commissioners decided should be conferred after examination in Civil Law, Scots Law, Conveyancing, Public Law, Constitutional Law and History, and Medical Jurisprudence. Candidates must be graduates in Arts, and the degree 'should be considered as a mark of academical and not of professional distinction'. For this reason the six examiners for the degree were expressly instructed to have special regard to the acquirements of the candidates in Public Law and Constitutional History–otherwise the degree would tend to be 'regarded as a mere test of professional knowledge'. Finally, the Commissioners saw no reason to interfere with the existing practice by which the higher degree of LLD was conferred 'as an honorary degree only'.

In all these decisions concerning the Law Faculty, the Commissioners were avowedly much influenced by the views of the Faculty of Advocates, and it soon became apparent that they had set their sights too high. The great mass of Law students, being destined to join the ranks of law agents and not of advocates, had purely professional training in view and very few of them had graduated in Arts before beginning their legal studies. In the first nine years of its existence only twenty-four students graduated LLB and the University Court introduced in 1874 an additional Law degree, the BL. Henceforth, the two degrees continued side by side, the BL being available for candidates who were not Arts graduates but had passed a 'satisfactory examination' in certain Arts subjects, and who preferred to devote themselves mainly to their professional studies in Civil Law, Scots Law, and Conveyancing, along with one of the other three subjects included in the LLB course. Although both degrees entitled the holders to a parliamentary vote after 1868, the BL was no more successful than the LLB in attracting candidates. Neither afforded any direct professional advantage and the law students who resorted to the University in ever increasing numbers preferred merely to attend the courses of instruction deemed necessary for their training.

In the Faculty of Divinity, alone of the existing faculties, the Commissioners found it impossible to legislate for the four universities and establish a degree which should be conferred after examination. The basic difficulty here was the Disruption of 1843, which split the Church of Scotland from top to bottom, and rendered obsolete the views of the Royal Commission of 1826 that, since the Divinity professors were necessarily members of the Church of Scotland, no provision need be made for students belonging to other denominations.

Before 1858 the Scottish universities were unanimous that members of other denominations should be entitled to take the degree of BD. The Free and United Presbyterian churches had already established their own Theological colleges, staffed by scholars of repute; and it would be contrary to the principles of religious toleration, as they were coming to be understood, to exclude students of these colleges from competing for Theological degrees. Glasgow, contrary to all the academic traditions of Scotland, wished to admit these candidates as external students to the degree examinations; Edinburgh and St Andrews, for once in agreement, would have required their attendance at university classes for one academic year; and Aberdeen proposed to institute in Divinity, but with elaborate theological safeguards, the same system of extra-mural teaching which had been so long a bone of contention in the Faculty of Medicine. For once the Commissioners were baffled by the intricacies of the question and decided to leave the universities to work out, unaided but unimpeded, their own solutions.

At Edinburgh, thanks to the initiative of the General Council, a Senatus decision of 1864 that candidates who were not members of the Church of Scotland must attend at least two qualifying courses for the BD degree at the University, was altered to admit Free Churchmen to the degree. Henceforth, the attendance required from candidates who were not Masters of Arts of Edinburgh University, could be in any two classes 'in one or more of the Faculties of the University'. At the same time the system introduced by the Commissioners of appointing examiners for degrees to act along with the professors was applied to the BD.

The Commissioners neither established a Faculty of Science, although the nucleus of such a faculty had long been in existence at Edinburgh, nor did they institute degrees in Science. The latter omission was remedied by the Senatus in 1864 when it introduced the degrees of Bachelor and Doctor of Science, which could be taken in the mathematical or in the physical or in the natural sciences. From 1870 these degrees could be conferred also in engineering and from 1874 in public health. The BSc degree in Agriculture was instituted in 1886. In addition, from 1864 candidates could present themselves for the degree of DSC in either Mental Science or Philology. Down to 1888 only sixty-five DSC degrees had in fact been conferred and twenty-one of these were in the one department of Physical Science; even the BSC had been awarded to no more than 224 candidates of whom sixty-six took the degree in Public Health in the same period. By comparison the newly instituted MB and CM degrees rose rapidly year by year until in the late 1880s more than 200 of each were conferred annually and in addition about fifty candidates obtained the higher standing of doctors of medicine each year. Whereas in 1859 only eighty-seven Edinburgh students, sixty-two of them medicals, had graduated, 617 took a degree in 1888.

The decisions of the Commissioners of 1858, judged as a whole, seem wise and statesmanlike; and Sir Alexander Grant, principal and historian of the University, wrote of 'the wave of prosperity which the Commission of 1858 set in motion' at Edinburgh. Contemporaries were less enthusiastic. Principal Brewster, addressing the students in 1860, was critical – the Commission did not have adequate powers to carry through reforms. The Faculty of Medicine protested against the medical ordinances issued by the Commissioners, and especially the encouragement given to extra-mural teaching. The General Council soon came to resent the narrow sphere of action to which it had been confined by the ordinances of the Commissioners and in particular clamoured for increased representation upon the University Court.

How far the rapid increase in the number of students in the next generation, which Grant attributed to the Act and Commission of 1858, was really due to them is debatable. The size of this increase can best be shown in tabular form:

Year	Faculty of Arts	Faculty of Divinity	Faculty of Law	Faculty of Medicine	TOTAL
1861–2	623	94	202	543	1462
1876–7	894	70	317	1070	2351
1885–6	1147	112	470	1873	3602
1887–8	992	100	492	1898	3482

While the Faculties of Arts and Law increased by about 50 per cent, Medicine doubled its numbers between 1861 and 1876. There was a steady rise in all faculties from 1877 to the peak year 1885–6, followed by a sudden drop in the Arts Faculty in the late 1880s. At Glasgow there was a smaller but comparable overall increase from 1,140 to 1,773 between 1861–2 and 1876–7, but here, although the small Faculty of Medicine rose by 50 per cent and the tiny Faculty of Law doubled its numbers, much the greatest increase was in Arts, which jumped from 631 to 1,113. At Aberdeen there was no substantial overall increase and at St Andrews the long drawn out process of decline continued. Since the four universities now had almost identical constitutions and very similar *curricula* for degrees, while class and other fees on the whole were lower at the two small universities than at Edinburgh and Glasgow, it is at first sight difficult to explain this state of affairs. No doubt the Medical Act of 1858 and the statutory recognition of Scottish degrees in Medicine and Surgery as qualifications to practise anywhere in the British dominions contributed to the resurgence of the Edinburgh Medical School and the rise of its younger sister at Glasgow; but it was the Commissioners who fought and won the battle against the medical corporations and effectively established these privileges in practice.

It would seem that the connection between the growth of the Arts Faculties and the Act and Commission of 1858 is less direct, except in so far as they awarded valuable privileges to students who took the MA degree and succeeded in making that degree more respected than it had hitherto been in England. The growth of the Arts Faculties at Edinburgh and Glasgow should probably be regarded as one aspect of Victorian prosperity, the rise of the middle classes, and the increasing opportunities available in Government service* and private enterprise for Arts graduates. The Commissioners, indeed, by insisting upon graduation in Arts before a student entered the Faculty of Law and by encouraging medical students to attend some Arts classes, set an example which was to be followed almost at once when the Bachelor's degree was instituted in Divinity. As other organised professions arose these examples were once again followed and it is only in the present decade that the Faculties of Divinity and Law have reversed their policies.

While the increasing belief that a liberal education in some Arts subjects should precede professional training made its effect felt in this period in the Faculty of Arts, at Edinburgh and to a less extent at Glasgow, it cannot explain the spectacular rise in the Glasgow Arts Faculty. So far as Arts was concerned, there was now a tendency for local boys to go to the local university; and, with the concentration of population in the Central Lowlands, this worked to the advantage of Glasgow and Edinburgh and to the disadvantage of the other universities. While Aberdeen had a sufficient hinterland and numerous

---

* For example, in the nineteen years ending with 1874, eighty-nine candidates from the Scottish universities entered the Indian Civil Service.

bursaries to attract local boys, St Andrews, after narrowly escaping annihilation, had to fall back upon English customers to fill its empty classrooms. At Edinburgh in the early 1860s, 400 of the 1,462 students had their homes in Edinburgh. Another 750 came from elsewhere in Scotland and the remaining 300 mainly from England and the British colonies.

The rapid development of secondary education in the Victorian era, which began in the cities and spread slowly in the landward areas from which Aberdeen and St Andrews drew most of their students, must also have contributed to the rapid expansion of the Edinburgh and Glasgow Arts Faculties. Whereas the schools which prepared boys for the universities in the eighteenth century taught them little but Latin and Mathematics, the new (or, like the Edinburgh High School, reorganised) secondary schools were now beginning to send up to the universities pupils conversant with the elements of a much wider range of school subjects. While this raised at the time in an acute form the old problem of the proper division of functions between the schools and the universities, and certainly made life difficult for the professors, who had to teach in one class some pupils educated under the old 'dominie system' and others from the advanced secondary schools, it also made possible the institution of honours degrees capable of standing comparison with those conferred by the English universities, old or new.

The Edinburgh Merchant Company by a redistribution of funds under its control established, to quote Grant, 'a splendid set of graded schools, of which the secondary schools for boys have been of special advantage to the University'. Moreover, by this time there were several private schools in Edinburgh fully capable of preparing boys for the universities, such as the Edinburgh Academy and the Edinburgh Institution, now known as Melville College. A minor factor in the Edinburgh Arts Faculty was presumably the creation of 'English public school' type establishments in the Edinburgh area. At least one of these, Fettes, was linked with the University by a system of exhibitions and fellowships. While the titles chosen for the awards indicated the anglicisation of these new schools, the scheme itself is comparable to the seventeenth-century arrangements made by George Heriot's hospital for its beneficiaries and others wishing to enter the University of Edinburgh.

At Edinburgh and Glasgow many of these Arts students were 'non-academical' or as we would now say 'non-graduating' students. Grant believed that 'perhaps out of the whole number of students joining the Arts Faculty the average length of attendance of each student at the University did not exceed two years. Thus the proportion of Arts students* graduating would be, up to [1883], about one to five or six'. Even so, the Commissioners had succeeded in increasing the proportion of Arts students who graduated. Whereas in the twenty years before the Commissioners' ordinances came into force at Edinburgh in 1863, only 250 M A degrees had been conferred, in the next twenty years 1,400 were awarded. Taking into account the steady increase in the number of Arts students between 1843 and 1883, it is obvious that a much larger proportion now took a degree at the end of their courses. The Representation of the People (Scotland) Act of 1868 gave a parliamentary vote to all graduates of the Scottish universities, and thus added substantially to the inducements to graduate which were already offered by the University Commissioners of 1858.

The Commissioners' attempt to encourage graduation with honours was a comparative failure. Only 176 of the 1,400 Arts graduates in the twenty years from 1863 to 1883 took honours, although appreciably more than half of the successful candidates were placed in the first class. Grant put his finger unerringly on the reason why so few candidates presented themselves for honours examinations–the Commissioners' requirement that all candidates for honours should previously have passed the whole examination for the ordinary degree. As early as 1867 the General Council, under the influence of Blackie, had recommended that candidates, who could show a fixed minimum knowledge of one of the subjects of the old seven-subject Arts curriculum, could substitute for it a subject chosen by themselves from a list consisting of Chemistry, Natural History, and Botany. In 1868, General Council, Senatus, and Court all agreed that candidates for the degree of M A with honours should not be required 'to go through the pass examination in that subject'; but this would have needed an alteration in the 1858 Commissioners' ordinance and did not become effective.

When the University Commissioners of 1876 reported on the Arts curriculum, they proposed a more radical departure from the 1858 line. Any candidate for honours who could pass a 'first examination' in Classics, Mathematics, English, and perhaps Science, would then be allowed to follow a specialised three-year course *either* in literature

---

* Including students enrolled in Engineering, Agriculture, Education, etc.

and philology *or* in philosophy *or* in Law and History *or* in Natural Science. Indeed this 'first examination' could also be used as a preliminary test in general culture for candidates who aspired to degrees in Law, Science, or Medicine, as well as to honours degrees in Arts. Also, to ensure that no unworthy student, possibly presented by a careless or partial private patron, continued to hold a bursary, the Commissioners recommended that all bursars, not later than a year after being elected to a bursary, should also have to pass the 'first examination'.

As the University Court recognised in 1880, such radical proposals for the reform of the seven-subject Arts curriculum would require parliamentary legislation and an additional government grant to compensate certain professors for their losses from student fees. The General Council received the proposals cordially and the Court took a step in the right direction by instituting, in 1880, 'Literate in Arts' certificates, which could be awarded to any student who passed at MA standard in five Arts subjects, provided that four of them were chosen from the seven compulsory MA subjects.

The need to raise standards, or at least not to lower them, was the principal argument used by the Commissioners of 1876 against the proposal to extend extra-mural teaching from Medicine to Arts and Law. Outside competition, they thought, with the professors in preparing students for degrees was a good thing in Medicine, where the primary object of the teaching was 'to impart information'. Applied to Arts, where 'the primary object of the teaching . . . is culture', degree examinations could not 'show that the student has cultivated his faculties in that way which it is the aim of his University training to ensure'. To introduce or extend the cramming system in Arts would force the professors in self-defence to lower their standards of teaching and narrow their treatment of their subjects to the bare minimum required to pass the degree examination.

VICTORIAN PROSPERITY

The granting of privileges to graduates, as Lorimer had foreseen, and particularly linking them for life to the University by means of the General Council, justified itself in another way. The Edinburgh

---

52. 'Our Principal Figure'–Sir William Muir; from *The Student*, 1891; one of a series of caricatures which purported to be suggestions for adorning the empty niches in the McEwan Hall.

University Property Arrangement Act had stripped the University of nearly all its old endowments; but its *alumni* (and other well-wishers) came to its aid and during the next thirty years bestowed one munificent endowment after another upon their *alma mater*. Dr John Muir founded the Chair of Sanskrit* and helped to found the 'Association for the better endowment of the University of Edinburgh' in 1864, which made known to a wider public the needs of the University. It had been recognised for a generation that the most urgent need was provision to enable outstanding students who had taken a degree to go on to post-graduate work. Prize essays and assistantships had both been advocated as means to this desirable end, but they were few in number and not altogether well adapted to secure the purpose in view. What was wanted was a reasonable subsistence for a fixed number of years which would enable the successful candidate to devote himself, without distractions, to further study. The Ferguson scholarships, established by a Glasgow merchant in 1861 and open to graduates of all the Scottish universities, were the first of a new kind of benefaction.

At Edinburgh in less than twenty years, sixteen such scholarships were established in the Arts Faculty, six scholarships or prizes in what would now be called the Faculty of Science, a similar number, though of less emolument, in Divinity and Medicine, and two in Law. In addition, Dr Vans Dunlop in 1879 left to the University a sum sufficient to provide eighteen scholarships, each of £100 a year for three years, nine in Arts, eight in Medicine, and one in Law. Competition for the new scholarships and prizes was not uniformly confined to graduates; but by the 1880s the University for the first time possessed the means to encourage the best of its graduates to proceed to further study and research. The prospect of winning one of these awards led students to specialise and must have contributed to the increasing popularity of honours degrees in the years that were to come. In Grant's opinion the effect of the new scholarships was most notable in Arts, where they 'produced higher work in some of [the Arts classes] than was before known in the University'.

In this same period many benefactors, amongst them Thomas Carlyle, established undergraduate bursaries of the traditional kind, but some of them were also influenced by the tendency towards

---

* Brother of Sir William Muir who was to succeed Sir Alexander Grant as principal in 1885.

specialised study. Carlyle, for example, directed that of the ten bursaries he founded in memory of his wife, five were to be awarded for proficiency in mathematics, and especially in pure geometry, and the other five for proficiency in classical learning. It is worth noting that Carlyle was convinced that mathematical ability would perennially offer 'in all epochs good promise for all manner of arts and pursuits', but had his doubts about classical learning or at least about the attitude of the Senatus to it in future years.

While at least £142,000 was given to the University for scholarships in the twenty years after 1862, an additional £90,000 was made available for bursaries. In preparing a scheme for throwing the arrangements connected with bursaries of all kinds at Edinburgh University 'into the form of a great annual ceremonial', the Senatus calculated in 1870 that the existing bursaries were worth £2,121 2s. 1d. *per annum*. Even so, Edinburgh remained much less well provided, in proportion to student numbers, with bursaries than Aberdeen, where in 1874 two-thirds of the Arts students were bursars, or St Andrews, of which it was popularly, but perhaps erroneously, believed in Edinburgh that there were more bursaries than students.

One symptom of a flourishing university is the rapid creation of new Chairs. Judged by this test Edinburgh prospered between 1858 and 1889. The foundation of the Sanskrit Chair in 1862 has already been mentioned. Six years later another private benefactor established the Chair of Engineering. The eminent geologist, Sir Roderick Murchison, provided funds in 1871 for a Chair of Geology. In each case the government undertook to subsidise the income of the new professor by an annual grant of £200. In the same year the Merchant Company founded a Chair of Political Economy and Mercantile Law; and in 1876 the Trustees of the Reverend Dr. Andrew Bell established at Edinburgh and St Andrews the first Chairs of Education in Great Britain, devoting to this purpose funds hitherto applied to subsidise elementary schools, which were now, as provided by the Education (Scotland) Act of 1872, to be supported from local rates. It was in connection with the Chair of Education that in 1886 there was instituted the first diploma to be awarded by the University to its graduates – the Schoolmaster's Diploma. In 1880 the Watson Gordon Chair of Fine Art was added by another private benefaction; and in 1881, after a long and arduous struggle in which Blackie took a prominent part, sufficient money was raised to endow the Chair of Celtic. It was expressly provided that as well as lecturing on Celtic

Philology and Antiquities, the new professor should give instruction in the 'uses and graces' of the Gaelic language. As Grant triumphantly pointed out only two new Chairs had been instituted at Edinburgh by private foundation in the 280 years down to 1862; in the next twenty years seven Chairs with an endowment of £58,000 from private sources had been established.

Edinburgh now had thirty-nine Chairs divided into the four Faculties of Arts (18), Medicine (12), Law (5), and Divinity (4). Students, who thought they were not receiving value for class fees paid to the professors, sometimes referred to them, with a disregard of arithmetical nicety, as the forty thieves. When to the benefactions for bursaries, scholarships, and Chairs are added those for the new Medical Buildings (£130,000) and for miscellaneous purposes, including the erection of a dome over the main entrance to the Old College (£14,000), the total private benefactions between 1863 and 1883 were, Grant thought, 'considerably understated' at £452,000. It should not be forgotten that, quite apart from benefactions, the increased number of students and the growing practice of graduation brought a substantial rise in University income. Matriculation fees rose from £1,496 in 1867 to £1,994 in 1876 and in the same period graduation fees rose from £1,756 to £3,110. By 1889 matriculation fees produced £3,479 and graduation fees £7,698.

It was no doubt natural that Grant, who shared as principal in the selection of professors appointed to old and new Chairs in this period, believed that the quality of the professors as a whole had never been so high. In considering this pronouncement it is only fair to point out that, especially in the Arts Faculty, they were being subjected to new and conflicting pressures which made their position more difficult than in the previous century. On the one hand they were being urged to produce scholars who could hold their own in Classics or Mathematics with the best that Oxford and Cambridge could produce; but every step taken in this direction was denounced by those who believed that the one end of a liberal education in Scotland was the study of divine philosophy. And other claims were already being vigorously put forward for adequate recognition of history, economics, modern languages, and other studies which were destined to become the basic Arts subjects of the twentieth century. Whatever subject he professed, there was now a rough and ready test which a professor's critics did not hesitate to apply—how did his pupils fair in open competitive examination for Indian and home Civil Service posts with the scholars

53. The Old Quad, showing Rowand Anderson's dome, Hutchison's figure of Youth (the 'Golden Boy'), and the Cumming fountain, from *The Student,* 1898–9.

produced by the old and new English universities and colleges? While
these problems were manifestly vital in the Arts Faculty, they were
not without significance also in the Faculty of Medicine, where the
Medical Act of 1858, and consequent changes in medical and surgical
teaching, made comparisons between English and Scottish medical
practitioners at once easier to make and more important.

The crux of these problems was how to compete successfully with
England without virtually closing the Scottish universities to the ill-
prepared lad of parts from a parish school or no school at all. How
could the professor of Greek, for example, hope to satisfy, in a single
course of lectures, the needs of the boy from the High School or the
Academy, who had already mastered the rudiments of the language,
and the uninstructed novices who were still struggling to learn the
alphabet? The institution of University assistantships helped, but by
no means solved this problem. The radical solution was to impose an
entrance examination and insist that those who could not pass at a
modest level must be drilled by the assistant before being admitted to
the class. Blackie adopted this; but his action was bitterly denounced
as an injustice to the bright but ill-prepared student, who could catch
up during the session with the rest of the class, and also as a breach of
the Scottish academic tradition of free entry for all to the universities.
Those who used the latter argument cannot have been aware that
what Blackie was now doing had, in fact, been done in the case of
Latin during the first session of the University nearly 300 years earlier.

Opinion, as manifested in General Council debates and in other
ways, moved steadily towards a compulsory entrance examination,
which had been deliberately rejected by the Commissioners of 1858.
Grant believed that the Arts professors of his day were 'set to do a
vast amount of work which was unworthy of them', because so many
of their students were so ill-prepared. The Commissioners of 1876,
while adhering to the belief that no student should be excluded from
the University by a preliminary examination, wished to introduce an
examination which could be taken before a candidate entered the
University, and which would give him valuable privileges if he passed,
including the right to specialise from the beginning of his course and
to take an honours degree in three years. This line of approach
proved in the end the most effective method of raising the standard
of 'Scotch degrees' to the level of those granted by English universities
in the same subjects. The General Council had no doubt that their
University should establish an examination for candidates from the

middle and upper schools of Scotland. Thus was instituted in 1865 the system of local examinations, intended 'to supply a common test of attainment both for pupils of public schools [in the Scottish sense] and for those privately educated'. Although this proved a great success for many years, it did not really fulfil the hopes of its promoters – out of a total of 891 candidates who were examined at forty-seven centres in 1883, 746 were girls.

This introduces another new problem which faced the professors of Queen Victoria's time. It is true that ladies had been admitted early in the nineteenth century to certain special courses of lectures given by individual professors on their own subjects within the College buildings; but attendance on such courses could not qualify them for degrees and the Senatus discontinued the experiment. In 1867, however, the 'Association for the Higher Education of Women' was founded in Edinburgh and soon changed its title to the 'Association for the University Education of Women'. While its more radical members advocated the admission of women to the University classes qualifying for degrees on equal terms with men, an intermediate course was in fact adopted. Some of the professors, each on his own subject, gave a special course of lectures for ladies only during the winter session. Some of these courses attracted as many as seventy or eighty students. The Association acquired a building of its own, with classrooms and a library, in which courses were regularly given in English Literature, Latin, Greek, Logic, Moral Philosophy, Political Economy, Theory of Education, Fine Art, and Mathematics, amongst the Arts subjects, and even in Biblical Criticism, Experimental Physics, Botany, Physiology, and Zoology. As a poor substitute for a degree, the University awarded from 1872 a 'certificate in Arts' to any lady who attended the Association's classes and passed in three subjects, provided that she had previously passed the Senior Local Examinations. Moreover, any candidate could subsequently present herself for examination at a higher level and obtain an 'honour certificate' in any one of her three subjects. It is not clear whether this relaxation of the Procrustean Arts curriculum for the benefit of the ladies contributed to the flexibility introduced into the old system by the 1889 Commissioners for male students who wished to graduate. What is curious is that a compulsory entrance examination was introduced for women before the principle was applied to men.

Less happy was the attempt to apply the principle of separate classes for women to the medical curriculum. When in 1869 Miss

Sophia Jex-Blake applied for permission to attend some of the medical classes, a majority of the Senatus were in favour of her application. The University Court then gave permission to any Medical professor who desired it to lecture on his subject to a group of ladies at a different hour from his graduating class of men. Several professors gave such courses and others were given by extra-mural teachers, one of whom with equal daring and folly, lectured to a mixed class of men and women. Miss Jex-Blake then found that the remaining professors, for one reason or another, declined to give special courses of lectures to the group of women students she had collected, who had already attended extra-murally all the courses which could be counted towards a medical degree under the ordinances. The Medical professors in 1874 claimed that they had done everything in their power for Miss Jex-Blake and her friends, but the University Court in 1875 petitioned the House of Commons against a bill intended to facilitate the education at Edinburgh of medical women. The attitude adopted at Edinburgh may be compared with the readiness of the University of London to accept in 1878 a supplemental charter making every degree, honour, and prize awarded by the university accessible to students of both sexes on equal terms. Finally Miss Jex-Blake sued the chancellor and Senatus Academicus of the University in the Court of Session, which, on appeal from the Lord Ordinary, held that the University had no power to admit women to degrees. Public sympathy had been aroused and, after a good deal of agitation, Parliament in 1889 authorised the universities to admit women to degrees.

THE PROFESSORS AND THEIR ASSISTANTS

A brief review of the professors who taught at Edinburgh in this period would on the whole confirm Grant's claim that as a body they were not inferior to any generation of their predecessors. They included Philip Kelland, a Cambridge graduate, who held the Chair of Mathematics from 1838–79 and was in Anglican orders, 'the first Englishman, with an entirely English education, who was ever appointed' to an Edinburgh Chair; Thomas Laycock, professor of the Practice of Physic (1855–76), the first Englishman who had received no part of his medical education in Scotland to be appointed to a Chair in the Faculty of Medicine; and John Hughes Bennett, another English-

54. Sophia Jex-Blake; painted by Samuel Lawrence.

man, who had however come to Edinburgh for his medical education, and who was well known for his opposition to excessive blood-letting and his advocacy of cod-liver oil. Principal Brewster and the great majority of the professors were still Scottish by origin and education. Principal Grant owed his education to Harrow and Oxford, but the great names on the roll of professors in the second half of the nineteenth century were mostly *alumni* of Edinburgh. Of the twenty professors selected for mention on account of their eminence in the following paragraphs, only two (Muirhead and Turner) had had no part of their education at a Scottish university and sixteen had studied at the University of Edinburgh. At least eight of them after a Scottish university course had gone abroad to study in France, Germany, or Switzerland. What was to become in the next generation the normal pattern of a Scottish university course followed by further study at Oxford or Cambridge was still quite exceptional.

In Arts these eminent professors included William Edmonstoune Aytoun, who transformed a declining Chair of Rhetoric into the pioneer Chair of English Literature in the British Isles, and his successor, David Masson, a fine scholar whose professional work still figures in the standard bibliographies. Masson left a lifelong impression upon his students, including my father, who as an old man was wont to quote from Masson's lectures on Milton and Shakespeare; and his work for the university education of women is kept green by the existence of Masson Hall. In Classics, Pillans, before his retirement from the Chair of Humanity in 1863, had greatly raised the standard and reorganised the teaching of Latin, and his work was ably continued by Sellar (1863-90). Their colleague Blackie, in the Greek Chair from 1852 to 1882, if less successful as a teacher of his subject, became a legend in his own life-time and did yeoman service for the University in other ways. Cosmo Innes, who held the Chair of History from 1846 to 1874, was the foremost record scholar of his generation and his editions of sources are still the everyday tools of the historian of Scotland. George Chrystal (Mathematics, 1879-1911) 'notably strengthened the reputation of Edinburgh as a centre of Mathematical research'.

Outstanding scientists who held Edinburgh Chairs were P. G. Tait (Natural Philosophy 1860-1901), 'one of the giants of Victorian physics' and joint author with Lord Kelvin of a famous text-book; Lyon Playfair and Crum Brown (Chemistry 1858-69 and 1869-1908), the latter reputed by his contemporaries to be capable of 'filling any

55. Professor J. S. Blackie hands over to his successor S. H. Butcher on the
steps leading to the rostrum in the Greek classroom; engraving by
William Hole from *Quasi Cursores*, 1884.

Professor CHR-ST-L,
who recently succeeded, amid a scene of unrivalled enthusiasm,
in making a correct addition.

Chair in the University'; and Wyville Thomson (Natural History 1870–82), best remembered for his share in the *Challenger* expedition which sailed round the world to examine the bed of the oceans and its fauna. Sir Archibald Geikie, the first professor of Geology (1871– 1881) did work which still commands respect. The most prominent of the lawyers were James Lorimer (Public Law 1862–90), the leading protagonist of University reform in the 1850s and 1860s, and James Muirhead (Civil Law 1862–89). Memorable amongst the professors in the Faculty of Divinity were Charteris (Biblical Criticism 1868– 1898), a pioneer in social work, and Flint (Divinity 1876–1903), whose lectures made a lasting impression upon his students and whose published works extended his influence to the world of scholarship.

Even an Arts man must however admit that the resurgence of the Faculty of Medicine was the most prominent feature of the academic history of the later nineteenth century. Of Robert Christison (Medical Jurisprudence 1822–32 and Materia Medica 1832–77) Grant remarked 'no professor, out of all the long list [since the foundation of the University] ever made so great an impression by his character on the University'. The cynic may be inclined to suggest that this was partly to be explained by his tenure of an Edinburgh Chair for fifty-five and a half years, which was then, is now, and seems likely to remain a record.

Christison had a chance to establish another record, but did not take it. On the accession of William IV in 1830, Professor Ballingall had been knighted as a reward for accompanying Principal Baird to London to present the address from the University to the new Sovereign. When Baird tried to press Ballingall's claim to a knighthood on the ground of his service as assistant-surgeon with the Duke of Kent's regiment, Peel retorted 'No, Mr Principal! on the ground of eminence among your professors solely, and on no other account'. Another Edinburgh professor, Leslie, was knighted shortly before his death in 1832 on the recommendation of Brougham, who seems also to have been responsible for the knighthoods conferred about the same time on Brewster and Charles Bell. Christison long afterwards claimed that he refused to go to London with the deputation and be named by the principal for the honour of knighthood because he 'held that no member of the medical profession ought to accept a knighthood put in his way in this accidental manner, or for any other

56. Professor George Chrystal; a caricature from *The Student,* 1909.

57. Professor James Syme, assisted by his staff and students, employed in reducing a dislocation of the shoulder (1825); from *The Student*, 1907.

reason than pure merit in medicine'. He had to wait therefore until 1871 when Gladstone personally, and 'in a peculiarly gracious manner', offered him a baronetcy 'as a compliment to [him] self, to the medical profession in Scotland, and to the University of Edinburgh'.

Even so, the glory of a hereditary title must have been slightly dimmed for Christison by the fact that his recent rival for the principalship of the University, J. Y. Simpson, had already achieved the same status in 1866. Sir William Hamilton and Sir Alexander Grant were both baronets but inherited their titles. Apart from Ballingall and Leslie, the first Edinburgh professor to be knighted during the tenure of his Chair seems to have been Henry R. Bishop (Music) in 1842. The first principal or professor to be raised to the peerage during his tenure of office at Edinburgh was Ritchie Calder, professor of International Relations, now, since 1966, Lord Ritchie-Calder.

Christison's colleague, Syme (Clinical Surgery 1833–69), was the foremost British, if not European, surgeon of his day. Dr John Brown said of him that he never wasted 'a word, a drop of ink, or a drop of blood'. Apart from his professional skill, he was a successful advocate of numerous reforms. Like Christison, he took a leading part in the struggle to overthrow town-council control of University patronage and administration. He was also a successful advocate of extra-mural teaching in Medicine, the Medical Act of 1858, and the rebuilding of the Royal Infirmary on the site which it still occupies. In spite of all this, I suspect that Syme nowadays is at best dimly known to students of surgical science. J. Y. Simpson (Midwifery 1840–70) did experimental work in the use of anaesthetics, and his successor, Syme's pupil and son-in-law Joseph Lister (Clinical Surgery 1869–77), in antiseptics, which 'completely revolutionised the practice of Surgery'

and secured for them a permanent and honourable place in the history of mankind. To this list, brief and incomplete as it is, must be added the name of William Turner (Chair of Anatomy 1867–1903, principal and vice-chancellor 1903–16), who is the only Edinburgh professor to become principal since George Baird was appointed in 1793, with the recent exceptions of Sir John Fraser and Professor Michael Swann.

Nevertheless, in the opinion of Comrie, author of the standard *History of Scottish Medicine,* 'the last quarter of the nineteenth century was, in regard to teaching in the University [of Edinburgh], rather a period of decline'. Large numbers of undergraduates preferred to go to extra-mural teachers and very few of the professors troubled to attract research workers to their laboratories. Comrie believed that the decline in medical teaching in the University was more than balanced by the 'exceptional brilliance' of extra-mural teaching at this time. There seems to be some inconsistency here since a considerable proportion of the Medical professors had previously taught extra-murally and were presumably appointed to Chairs because of their proved ability to teach undergraduates and to conduct research. In 1884 the Edinburgh Colleges of Physicians and Surgeons joined with the Glasgow Faculty of Physicians and Surgeons to examine and grant to successful candidates the so-called triple qualification to practise as physicians and surgeons. Another important factor in medical progress at this time was the Royal Medical Society originally established in 1737.

After weighing the arguments on both sides it is hard to resist the conclusion that one major cause of increased numbers, at least in Arts and Medicine, was the eminence of the professors and the skill and enthusiasm with which they discharged their duties. Whereas in the eighteenth century a professor who was a good and assiduous teacher was deemed a success, it was now coming to be recognised that, under changed conditions, no professor who was not himself engaged in advancing the bounds of his subject could hope to be a satisfactory teacher. Conservative fears that to increase professorial salaries and to diminish the importance of class fees in remunerating the professors would reduce the teaching efficiency of the University proved ill-founded. And the ablest of the professors still found time to play their part outside of the University in various activities such as the Lecture-Extension Association, founded in 1888 to provide academic lecture courses for persons unable to attend the University.

The increase in student numbers, to whatever cause it should be attributed, raised grave problems. The labour of correcting written work, as Aytoun found when his class rose from 30 to 150 in the course of a few years, proved almost insupportable. Those professors who were not provided with University assistants were forced to delegate part of this duty to assistants who were appointed and paid by themselves. Usually these men were selected from the best students in the class in previous years. Such appointments were often useful in supplementing the income of young graduates who had won scholarships or prizes, but the system was liable to abuse. The 1876 Commissioners were favourably impressed by the work done by the assistants and recommended that, if class fees were raised—and most of them had remained unaltered for more than half a century—the additional revenue should be devoted partly 'to the better remuneration of the class assistants [especially for large classes] or the provision of additional assistants'. By 1876–7 tutorial or laboratory classes conducted by them already existed in Humanity, Greek, Mathematics, Natural Philosophy, Astronomy, Clinical Medicine, and Anatomy.

Enlightened professors no longer believed that a student capable of reproducing their lecture notes with reasonable accuracy was entitled to a pass in the degree examinations. The University Library, with probably only one copy of the standard texts, though the Commissioners of 1858 believed that it was serving students better than any of the other university libraries in Scotland, could do little to help the class of over two hundred students who attended Humanity or Natural Philosophy in 1876–7 and the even larger classes of Natural History (411) and Chemistry (264), not to mention the 435 students who attended the practical Anatomy class in the same winter session. One answer to this particular difficulty, at least so far as it concerned the large Arts classes, was the provision of class or departmental libraries; and here Pillans was a pioneer.

In the large medical and scientific classes even more serious problems arose, when an increasing number of students were required to undertake individual practical work in conjunction with the lectures and demonstrations given by the professor. To meet the needs of supervision and guidance, new categories of student-assistants, demonstrators, and technicians painfully evolved in the Faculties of Arts (which still included in embryo most of the Science Faculty), Medicine, and Law, but not in Divinity. By 1876 there were already ten assistants in Arts, six in Law, and twenty-nine in Medicine. Most of them were appointed by the professor with the sanction of Senatus. Some were paid out of public moneys and some by the professors out of their own pockets, but most of them received a salary from the General University Fund. Their duties varied from department to department. Whereas in Arts they were mainly employed in correcting written work and conducting tutorial classes, in Medicine and Science they were chiefly engaged in preparing and giving demonstrations and superintending students' practical work in the laboratories. A few were already partly occupied in conducting classes which did not form part of the professor's qualifying class for a degree, and which were often held in the summer session.

Another development of even greater significance was the beginning of the lecturer grade. In accordance with the views of the Royal Commission of 1876, which believed that a new subject of instruction need not necessarily require a new professor to teach it, two or three specialised lectureships had come into existence before 1889. These included one on diseases of the eye and another on mental diseases, as well as a special lectureship in Natural Theology, endowed by Lord Gifford in each of the Scottish universities. Lectureships, unlike professorships, need not be permanent appointments and the Commissioners thought that 'in many respects it may be advantageous for the universities to be unfettered in their power of extending and strengthening their means of instruction' by appointing lecturers who would not add to the membership of Senatus, already inconveniently large at Edinburgh. Partly for this reason, they wished to restrict still further the right of the Scottish universities to establish new Chairs by making necessary the previous consent of a General University Court, containing representatives of each university along with nominees of the Crown, which it proposed should be established. Taken together these attempts to cope with pedagogic problems were clearly inadequate in the period down to 1889; but they pointed the ways in which progress was ultimately to be made. Needless to say, the adoption of new lines of approach to old problems created fresh difficulties which are still with us in 1966.

NEW BUILDINGS

Increasing numbers of students raised again the old bogey of accommodation. In 1858 the Old College building was already becoming inadequate, although student numbers had dropped from the post-

Napoleonic war peak. The Adam-Playfair buildings made no provision as had been intended for subsidiary needs, such as a College chapel, graduation hall, or professors' houses; but for a generation they did provide class accommodation up to date in construction and sufficient in quantity. The only addition, in fact, made to them in over half a century was the belated construction, out of the income of the Reid bequest, after long litigation in the Court of Session between the professor of Music and the Senatus, of the Music Classroom, fitted with an organ of suitable size and quality. The provision of this classroom in Park Place, some distance away from the Old College, was the first step in a process which has scattered the University buildings widely in different parts of the town and even beyond the city boundaries. While the Senatus, in December 1858, ordered that the foundation stone of the Music Classroom should be laid 'with as little ceremony as possible', Donaldson, the triumphant professor of Music, when the building was completed in 1860, gave a banquet in the Corn Exchange, to which he invited all the workmen who had been employed in the work of construction.

The vast increase in student numbers after 1858 gave urgency to the problem of class accommodation. Since a much larger percentage of students now graduated, it was no longer possible to conduct the laureation ceremony in the Chemistry classroom. Outside halls, such as the Assembly Hall, had now to be hired on each occasion. Voices were therefore raised in the General Council in favour of a graduation hall, which could also be used for the formal mass examinations which had now become a regular routine in the four faculties. An abortive attempt was made to link the provision of a graduation hall with the commemoration of the hundredth anniversary of the birth of Sir Walter Scott.

Other graduates urged the need for a University chapel, but the University authorities rightly gave priority to the provision of a new quadrangle, devoted entirely to medical teaching and research. From the standpoint of the other faculties, this solution was warmly approved, partly at least because it would enable them to secure the additional accommodation they badly required on the old site and, at the same time, rid them of neighbours, who were not always congenial, and whose professional pursuits sometimes offended the more delicate olfactory organs of the Faculties of Arts, Divinity, and Law. The rapid succession of new non-medical Chairs founded after 1858 intensified the problem of accommodation. There was also a general recognition that if the resurgent Medical Faculty was to continue to hold its place as one of the leading medical schools of the world, it must have not merely classrooms large enough to contain its students, but new laboratories, museums, and theatres equipped with up-to-date apparatus for teaching and research, and housed in buildings immediately adjacent to the Royal Infirmary.

As early as 1869 a public meeting was called and the required site, across the Middle Meadow Walk from the new Royal Infirmary, was purchased at a cost of £33,000, to which a timely legacy from Sir David Baxter contributed £18,000. The first public appeal in 1874 raised only £60,000; but six Edinburgh architects were invited to submit plans for a Medical School which would provide all the accommodation required by the professors of Anatomy, Institutes of Medicine, Practice of Physic, Surgery, Midwifery, Pathology, Materia Medica, and Medical Jurisprudence. When these professors were consulted about the plans, 'a considerable majority' thought that those of Robert Rowand Anderson were most satisfactory; and the Committee, being convinced that his elevations 'were, on the whole, the most elegant and tasteful' as well as functionally sound, appointed him as their architect. His original plans included a graduation hall to accommodate 3,000 persons, and an Italian *campanile*.

When the Committee, in 1874, applied, in accordance with precedent, for a government grant, they informed the Treasury that the metropolitan University of Scotland 'has long contained the largest and most important medical school in the United Kingdom'. This school was 'by no means wholly, or even chiefly, Scotch, but is national, or rather imperial, in character'. In 1874–5 the birth-places of the medical students showed 369 Scots, 333 English, 21 Irish, 57 born in India, 97 in the colonies, and 48 in other countries. The appeal was further buttressed by quotations from the Act of Union of 1707 and from the more recent Seventh Report of the Royal Commission on Scientific Instruction (1875), which had recommended increased assistance to the University from government funds, provided that, in accordance with precedents set in the cases of Colleges in London and Manchester, 'the grant of a capital sum in aid of the extension of the University should be contingent upon the receipt of substantial contributions from private sources'. Moreover a closer neighbour than Owen's College and the Metropolitan Colleges of London had already received £120,000 towards the erection of new buildings at Glasgow on Gilmorehill. Edinburgh's claim was strongly supported by the Royal Commission on the Scottish universities, which reported in 1878 that the plans and designs 'have been prepared on a moderate scale and with a careful regard to economy'.

While they admitted Edinburgh's claim to assistance in principle, the Treasury Lords insisted that the hall and the tower must be excised from Anderson's original plan. This brought the estimated cost of the new building down to £180,000, towards which £80,000 had now been raised. If an additional £20,000 could be raised, the Treasury agreed to provide £80,000 from public money. A new appeal soon produced the additional £20,000 and the work of construction began. It was only then that the Committee discovered that what the professors had deemed sufficient in 1874 was quite inadequate to their needs in the 1880s. Parts of the building already constructed had to be demolished and changes made in the plans to accommodate the greatly increased numbers of students, while internal alterations were also required to save the Medical Faculty from starting its new career in what the Medical professors now considered a substandard building.

Finally, the additional sum required was raised by a 'Tercentenary appeal' in 1883; but even the enthusiasm shown at the Tercentenary celebrations failed to provide money for an academic hall. Grant remarked sorrowfully that all the ceremonies connected with the Tercentenary would have to be 'conducted in some hired apartment'. Not until 1897, and by the private munificence of William McEwan, MP was this long-standing need met. In 1887 the Old Quadrangle was embellished by the erection of a dome, designed by Rowand Anderson, over the main entrance and on top of the dome stands a gilded statue of youth. This statue, the work of John Hutchison RSA, was placed in position in 1888 and paid for from a surplus in the Robert Cox bequest after the completion of the dome. These additions have been criticised by some purists as a departure from Adam's plan. Nevertheless, the whole grouping, especially when illuminated on occasions of academic junketing, makes an effective finish to the Adam-Playfair building, and introduces an element of lightness and romanticism to its massive and severely classical architecture.

STUDENT LIFE

Little need be said about student life and manners in this period. In 1859 when there was a widespread fear of French invasion, a group of students led by the senior professor, Christison, formed a University

Company of Volunteers for home defence, which drilled in the Old Quadrangle and skirmished over Arthur Seat. In retrospect the most important event was the establishment in 1884 of the Students Representative Council. Conceived by Robert Fitzroy Bell and at once welcomed by the University authorities, it at first devoted its energies mainly to promote social life and academic unity among the students. Within a few years it had worked strenuously and successfully (1) to establish the University Union, which opened its first session in October 1889; (2) to make adequate provision for University athletics; and (3) to create, in place of ephemeral periodicals such as the *Edinburgh University Magazine* of 1871, in which Robert Louis Stevenson first appeared in print, a University magazine which should be 'the permanent interpreter of student opinion'. When R. C. Buist, who founded *The Student* in November 1887, left the University, the SRC, in May 1888, 'adopted *The Student* as its official journal'. Success in these projects allowed the Council, which had been speedily copied by the students of other Scottish universities, to devote more attention to other aims which it had envisaged from its very beginning, especially the representation of the general body of students and the provision of a recognised means of communication between the student body and the University authorities.

To the meeting which led to the creation of the SRC, Bell had summoned the presidents and secretaries of all the University societies, which continued to flourish side by side with the new institution. The support of these societies contributed to the success of the SRC, while the SRC not only provided a forum for discussion of student needs and a focus for student action, but encouraged the formation of new societies to meet the expanding diversification of student interests.

The SRC may be regarded as the outstanding sign of Victorian prosperity and middle-class self-confidence amongst the student body, but it does not stand alone. Every decade of Victoria's reign offered to the students increased opportunities of recreation and entertainment, plays, pantomimes, concerts, visits to the Edinburgh Aquarium or the Royal Gymnasium with its wrestling ring 'laid with bark', its shower baths, 'now considered an indispensable auxiliary', lavatory, reading-room, etc. The Senatus was soon to abandon the prohibition, which it had maintained for nearly two centuries, against students taking part in amateur production of plays. With the rapid growth of the town, more and probably better lodgings became available for students, most of whom could now afford to pay more for food and lodging than their Scottish predecessors in the eighteenth century. University Hall, founded in 1887 by Patrick Geddes, then assistant to the professor of Botany, and endowed with rights of self-government, was intended to provide 'the long felt need in Scottish Universities of College life as understood in England with its social advantages and avoidance of the drawbacks of solitary life in lodgings'.* The 'poor student' was still prominent, but he had greatly extended opportunities of remunerative employment and successive University Commissions tenderly looked after his interests. The substantial increase of bursaries and prizes at Edinburgh, although the competition for them became ever keener, must also have done something to reduce utter penury.

The Students' Club, instituted in 1876 in its own rooms opposite the University, provided dinners for its members—two courses for one shilling—and numerous other facilities, which made it the ancestor of the University Union. Amongst the few attempts to cater officially for the material needs of students was the proposal of the General Council in 1866 to establish a students' refectory in the University. The professors spiked the guns of the Council by themselves taking steps 'to provide a refreshment room for the students'. In addition they set aside the Agricultural Hall in the Old College for gymnastics. How long these arrangements lasted cannot easily be determined; but they had perhaps ceased before the Tercentenary festival when Grant had his vision of George Square surrounded by 500 student residences and provided with a restaurant to supply their needs. More permanent was the provision in the Old Quadrangle, through the liberality of Mr Hope, of 'two beautiful commemorative fountains†
. . . where the students would have an ample supply of excellent drinking water'. They need no longer resort to the neighbouring public houses to wash down with beer and spirits their midday 'pieces'. These fountains still adorn the Old Quadrangle but the Cumming fountain, erected in 1886, was removed after the First World War to King's Buildings.

Much more important than this symptom of Victorian temperance in its effect on student life was the development of the Victorian cult of competitive team games. Unofficial groups of students began to

---

* An attempt in the 1860s to found, under the Limited Liabilities Act, an Edinburgh College Hall seems to have been still-born.
† They commemorate the tenure of the Chemistry Chair by the donor's uncle, Thomas Charles Hope, from 1795 to 1844.

play rugby and association football, cricket and golf, and other games. As early as 1866 an athletic club was formed and the first annual sports were held at Greenhill Park. In the following year the Alexandra Amateur Rowing Club changed its name to the University Boat Club. In 1871 the first Inter-University Sports were held at Edinburgh. In 1876 a University playing field was secured at Corstorphine and the University began to field official teams. Following upon the foundation of Rugby and Cricket Clubs in 1871, the Association Football Club was formed in 1878, its first team including three former pupils of Ayr Academy. The Bicycle Club was instituted in 1879, the Golf Club in 1881, and the Swimming Club in 1888. In 1887 the first Cambridge University rugby side to play in Scotland was defeated by an Edinburgh University team; and two years later the Edinburgh students lost a contest in racing and field events with the United Hospitals of London by three events to six. The SRC gave a powerful impulse to student athletics and in doing so unwittingly strengthened the already powerful trend towards the anglicisation of the University.*

It cannot be said that the reformed University of the later nineteenth century produced such a crop of outstanding men as its unreformed predecessor had done in the eighteenth and early nineteenth centuries. The annotated list of graduates from 1859 to 1888, which was published by order of the Senatus in 1889, shows that many of them reached positions of professional eminence as professors, physicians, surgeons, medical officers of health, inspectors of schools, administrative, scientific and medical civil servants, and principals of colleges and headmasters in Scotland, England, and overseas. Palmerston and Russell remained the only men who had been educated mainly at Edinburgh to become Prime Ministers of Great Britain. Even second-rate politicians are hard to come by after the demise of these two dreadful old men, as Queen Victoria, in a moment of exasperation, styled them. The Scottish nobility, with rare exceptions, had long ceased to send their sons to Scottish universities and the English nobility no longer had any inducement to do so. Since nobility of birth was still the surest and certainly the easiest avenue of approach to political eminence, the absence of Edinburgh men in the front rank, until the emergence of Haldane, is not surprising. An Edin-

---

* For further information on University athletics, reference should be made to Colonel C. M. Usher's *The Story of Edinburgh University Athletic Club* (Edinburgh, 1966).

58. A student athlete and a graduand; from *The Edinburgh University Quarterly*,
1882, the latter being part of an advertisement for Christie and Kirkpatrick,
at that time University outfitters and tailors on the South Bridge.

burgh medical graduate, Sir Charles Tupper, after a long career in
Canadian politics, became Premier of the Dominion in 1896.

In law the University continued to produce many eminent Scottish
judges, but none of her *alumni* sat on the Woolsack as Loughborough
and Brougham had done in the preceding period. The massive infil-
tration of Edinburgh graduates into the Civil Service had hardly
begun and it was the next generation of students who were to find
fame, if not fortune, in serving the Crown as administrators at home
and overseas. Even in literature, apart from Stevenson, Conan Doyle,
and Crockett, the period from 1858 to 1889 is almost a blank. Carlyle
was the last Edinburgh-educated historian to achieve fame. The days
when Edinburgh philosophers, such as Hume and Dugald Stewart,
had been household names all over Europe were no more. In the
register of scientific discoveries and inventions carried out in the later
nineteenth and early twentieth centuries, Edinburgh-trained scientists

played a minor role. Sir Alfred Ewing, however, lived to be principal
of his own University and, by enabling the United States Government to decipher a telegram from the German diplomatic agent to
Mexico, contributed to bring the United States into the First World
War. Only in Medicine and Surgery did the University continue to
produce practitioners of the highest quality. On the other hand, two
of the reigning Sovereign's sons signed the University matriculation
album, and while the Prince of Wales, later to reign as Edward vii,
was in fact instructed solely by the rector of the High School, his
younger brother, the Duke of Edinburgh, did attend the University
classes in Chemistry, Natural Philosophy, Natural History, and
History during the session 1863–4.

It may be said that this comparison is unfair to the generation of
students who attended the University in the middle years of Queen
Victoria's reign since it uses, for purposes of comparison, the achieve-
ments of their predecessors over the century from Hume to Carlyle.
On the other hand, the number of Edinburgh *alumni* in the thirty
years from 1858 to 1889 was probably not much less than that of
their predecessors from say 1720 to 1800. In the last resort, the paucity
of great names can perhaps be best explained on the lines of the
proverb about the wind blowing whither it listeth. Genius is inexplic-
able and in any case usually owes little to academic education. Hume
reacted violently against the teaching of his Edinburgh professors of
Philosophy and Scott was denounced as a dunce by one of the best
and ablest of his professors, Andrew Dalzel. What can safely be said
is that the University made a substantial and significant contribution
to the educated man-power of the British empire in the later nineteenth century.

NOTE ON SOURCES

ACKNOWLEDGEMENTS

INDEX

For the period down to 1646 Thomas Craufurd's *History of the University of Edinburgh* (Edinburgh, 1808) is invaluable. Andrew Dalzel's *History of the University of Edinburgh from its foundation*, ed. David Laing (Edinburgh, 1862), carries the story forward to 1723. Both adopt a strictly annalistic method and both had access to original sources no longer extant. Also useful, especially for biographies of professors and principals, is Alexander Bower's *History of the University of Edinburgh* (3 vols., Edinburgh, 1817–30); and the same author's *The Edinburgh Student's Guide* (Edinburgh, 1822) offers a contemporary account of the teaching available early in the nineteenth century. Sir Alexander Grant's *Story of the University of Edinburgh during its first three hundred years* (2 vols., London, 1884) was the first attempt to present a continuous narrative. In this it failed, but the numerous appendices present a comprehensive survey of the particular topics selected for historical treatment, while the general chapters offer authoritative comment on the problems of the University in the reign of Queen Victoria. The volume of *Charters, statutes, and acts of the town council and senatus 1583–1858*, ed. A. Morgan (Edinburgh, 1937), contains a judicious selection from one category of primary-source material for the history of the University. The collection of essays, *University of Edinburgh. Three hundred and fiftieth anniversary 1583–1933*, ed. A. Logan Turner (Edinburgh, 1933), lies almost entirely outside of the period which I have treated in this volume; the *University of Edinburgh Journal*, on the other hand, contains much relevant and valuable material.

Apart from these and other less valuable printed sources, this history is based on the voluminous collections of manuscript materials available in the archives of the University and of Edinburgh Corporation, supplemented occasionally by reference to the Scottish Record Office, the National Library of Scotland, and the British Museum. It has not been thought necessary to supply the reader of a short and 'popular' history with exact references, although a few have been added to books and articles with which he is less likely to be acquainted.

D.B.H.

ACKNOWLEDGEMENTS

The publishers are grateful to the following individuals and institutions for their kind permission to reproduce original paintings and drawings in this book :

Sir John Clerk, Bt. of Penicuik : 5

Colonel The Earl of Stair, CVO, MBE : 19

The Old Edinburgh Club : 42

The City Librarian : 2, 28, 41 (from the Edinburgh Room of the Central Public Library)

The Scottish National Portrait Gallery : 1, 4, 20, 21, 26, 27, 29, 35

The University of Edinburgh : 3, 6, 7, 8, 9, 10, 11, 12, 13, 14, 15, 16, 17, 18, 22, 25, 30, 31, 32, 36, 37, 38, 39, 40, 43, 44, 45, 46, 47, 48, 49, 50, 51, 52, 53, 54, 55, 56, 57, 58

Index